W9-BJM-111

STORIES IN HISTORY

A CHANGING
AMERICA

1865–1900

Cover illustration: Todd Leonardo

Printed in the United States of America

ISBN 0-618-14210-X

1 2 3 4 5 6 7 — QKT — 06 05 04 03 02 01

Table of Contents

*A number of African Americans held public
office in the Reconstruction South. Pinckney
Benton Stewart Pinchback became America's
first black governor. This is his story and the
story of the era that produced him.*

*Henry's father works for Ida B. Wells, the black
newspaper editor who exposes the horrors of
lynchings to a national audience. He asks her
what they can do. Henry is in trouble.*

PART III: INDUSTRIALIZATION AND THE END OF THE FRONTIER

About this Book

The stories are historical fiction. They are based on historical fact, but some of the characters and events may be fictional. In the Sources section you'll learn which is which and where the information came from.

The illustrations are all historical. Original documents help you understand the time period. Maps let you know where things were.

Items explained in People and Terms to Know are repeated in the Glossary. Look there if you come across a name or term you don't know.

If you would like to read more about these exciting times, you will find recommendations in Reading on Your Own.

Background

*If the Negro can not stand on his own legs,
let him fall.
. . . All I ask is, give him a chance to stand on
his own legs!*

—Frederick Douglass,
"What the Black Man Wants" (1865)

▲
Young African Americans learn to build carriages at Tuskegee Institute in Alabama.

Changes in the South

In the years following the Civil War's end in 1865, the South went through many difficulties.

Reconstruction

When Abraham Lincoln died, Andrew Johnson became president. There was a lot of work to be done. Important questions needed answers. How should the defeated Confederate states be admitted back into the Union? What should state government be like in the states that had fought the Union? How would the newly freed African Americans get the things they needed to live?

For twelve years after the Civil War, the U.S. government set policies for the South. This period, from 1865 to 1877, is called Reconstruction. During this time, the Fourteenth and Fifteenth Amendments to the Constitution were passed. These assured that no one could be kept from voting because of race or because of having once been a slave. Congress set up a Freedmen's Bureau to train teachers and build schools and hospitals for the former slaves.

▲

This 1881 print shows three African-American leaders of the Reconstruction Era: (left to right) Blanche K. Bruce, Frederick Douglass, and Hiram Revels. Bruce and Revels were each elected senator from Mississippi.

New Leaders in the South

The Fourteenth Amendment made it very difficult for any man who had been a leader in the Confederacy to hold political office. This meant that men from the old Southern families who had always been powerful could no longer run the government. They could not be governors or legislators. They could not be members of Congress.

For several years after the Civil War, the Republican Party dominated American politics. In the 1868 presidential election, about a half million African Americans in the South voted. They helped to elect the Republican candidate, Civil War hero Ulysses S. Grant. Also, for the first time, African Americans held political office in local, state, and federal positions. Sixteen were elected to the U. S. Congress.

Joining them in the new Republican governments were Northerners who came South after the war. Some sincerely wished to rebuild the South and help the former slaves. Others wanted to gain riches and power.

African Americans in the South

During Reconstruction, African Americans enjoyed new freedoms. Many traveled, reunited their families, and set up schools and churches. They founded black colleges and volunteer organizations. But years of slavery had left serious problems. Only ten percent of African Americans could read and write. Most had no land, money, or possessions. To earn a living, most worked as sharecroppers. They kept only a small portion of the crops they raised.

Violence against blacks did not end with the end of slavery. In 1866, former Confederate soldiers founded a secret organization of white men called the Ku Klux Klan. The Klan terrorized blacks and anyone who helped them. The U.S. government outlawed the Klan in the 1870s, but attacks continued.

▲
The Ku Klux Klan attacks an African-American family in their home.

Jim Crow Laws

In the 1870s, Reconstruction ended. In 1872, Congress passed a law allowing former Confederates to hold office again. Democrats began to recapture Southern state governments.

Once Democrats got control again, they passed laws restricting blacks and shutting down schools and social programs. Throughout the South, Democrats set up "Jim Crow" laws that separated African Americans from white society. In 1896, in a case called *Plessy* v. *Ferguson*, the U.S. Supreme Court said separate facilities were legal. This Supreme Court ruling wasn't reversed until 1954.

Western Expansion

> *Go West, young man, and grow up with the country.*
> —Horace Greeley (1850)

Millions of people settled in the American West between 1865 and 1900. They turned 400 million acres of Western land into farms. Government programs helped this growth.

Settlers

In 1862, Congress passed the Homestead Act. This law gave families 160 acres of land in the Great

Plains if they were willing to work it for five years. Between 1862 and 1900, the Homestead Act brought between 400,000 and 600,000 families to the Great Plains. In other areas of the West, land was sold cheaply or given away. Demand for this land was high. In an 1889 Oklahoma land giveaway, new settlers claimed two million acres in 24 hours.

The government encouraged the building of railroads by giving loans and over 170 million acres of land to four railroad companies. By 1869, a railroad had been built across the West. This line linked up with railroads in the East to form a transcontinental system stretching across the United States. Settlers who could afford it could travel across the West in comfort at 50 miles an hour. (A "bargain" fare from Omaha, Nebraska, to Sacramento, California, was $40—more than a month's pay for the average person.) Railroads also opened new markets across the country.

Native Americans

As white settlers moved west, they came into conflict with Native Americans. Some tribes had lived in the West for thousands of years. Other tribes had been pushed west by treaties with the U.S. government.

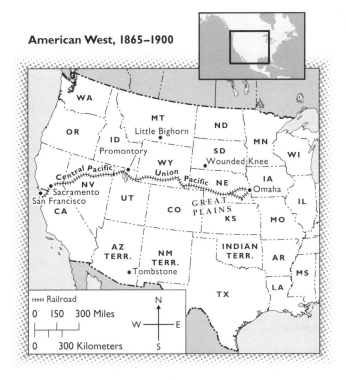

American West, 1865–1900

After the Civil War, the government broke its earlier treaties with the Native Americans and signed new ones, moving the tribes into smaller areas. Some tribes—like the Cheyenne, Sioux, Kiowa, and Comanche—resisted signing these treaties. They became angry as they saw white hunters almost wipe out the 20 million buffalo on which the Plains Indians' way of life depended. Native Americans attacked settlers, wagon trains, and railroads. The government sent in the U.S. army to protect the settlers. Through wars and mass killings, the army finally drove all of the remaining Native Americans onto reservations.

On reservations, Native Americans had few rights and lived in poverty. Government-run schools were set up to teach native children to reject their cultures and adopt white ways. The Dawes Act, passed in 1887, also tried to force Native Americans to change their traditional ways of life by dividing reservations into individual plots of land for each family. However, this effort largely failed because most Native Americans lacked the resources to be successful farmers.

Growth of Industry and Wealth

Success. Four flights. Thursday morning. All against twenty-one mile wind. Started from level with engine power alone. Average speed through air thirty-one miles. Longest fifty-nine seconds. Inform press. Home Christmas.

—Orville and Wilbur Wright,
telegram describing first airplane flight (1903)

When the Civil War ended in 1865, America was mostly a rural nation. By 1920, it had become the world's leading industrial power. This boom in industry was due to natural resources, an explosion of inventions, and a growing urban market for new products.

Natural Resources

Coal and oil were America's most important natural resources during this period. In 1859, the use of steam power made it practical to drill for oil. This new technology set off an oil boom. Oil and coal were used to make kerosene for lighting lamps. In 1856, the Bessemer process for producing steel was developed. Steel was strong and lightweight and had many uses. Among them were railroad tracks, barbed wire, farm machines, and tin-plated cans. Steel frames made huge structures like the Brooklyn Bridge and skyscrapers possible.

◀ The power of American industry in the late 1800s is expressed in this picture of Bessemer converters in a steel mill.

Inventions

Many key inventions and discoveries were made between 1865 and 1900.

Edison's system for producing and distributing electricity led to America's growth. This low-cost, convenient form of energy powered appliances, streetcars, and industrial plants. Telephones and typewriters opened up new office jobs which were mainly filled by women. Invention of the sewing machine helped build new clothing industries, which also employed many women. The following are some key inventions of this period:

1846—Sewing machine (Elias Howe)

1852—Elevator: makes skyscrapers practical (Elisha G. Otis)

1867—Typewriter (Christopher Shoales)

1869—Vacuum cleaner (I. W. McGaffey)

1874—Barbed wire: fences cattle out of crops, making farming possible in treeless Great Plains (Joseph F. Glidden)

1876—Telephone (Alexander Graham Bell and Thomas Watson)

1878—Phonograph (Thomas Edison)

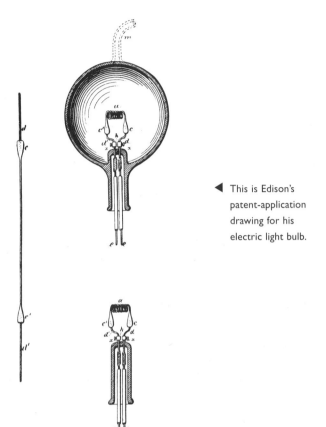

◀ This is Edison's patent-application drawing for his electric light bulb.

1879—Electric light bulb (Edison)

1882—First large-scale electric power station (Edison)

1886—Linotype machine: makes mass-circulation newspapers practical (Ottmar Mergenthaler)

1903—First airplane flight (Wright Brothers)

Urban Markets

The railroads unified the nation and helped to create new towns and cities. Now, goods and products could be shipped across the nation to new urban markets.

Iron, coal, steel, lumber, and glass industries grew rapidly. In a world of free competition, some businessmen—called "robber barons"—ignored laws and grew rich. Among them were Cornelius Vanderbilt (shipping and railroads), Andrew Carnegie (steel), and John D. Rockefeller (oil). In 1890, Congress passed the Sherman Anti-Trust Act in an attempt to control business activities.

Between 1869 and 1914, America's wealth grew four times larger. The problem was that the wealth resulting from the expanding American economy was distributed very unequally. Although their wages increased, much of the working class remained very poor. In 1890, the richest one percent in the United States earned more than the bottom 50 percent. The wealth of this same top one percent was greater that that of the other 99 percent of the American people.

Changes in Society

Immigration

Give me your tired, your poor,
Your huddled masses yearning to breathe free, . . .

—Emma Lazarus,
words on the Statue of Liberty (1883)

In 1848, the discovery of gold in California set off a Gold Rush that drew thousands of Chinese immigrants to the West Coast. The Japanese came there later, seeking work.

In Europe, land was scarce and poor people had few opportunities. When American railroads offered to sell land for $6 per acre, many Europeans thought their dreams had come true. Between 1870 and 1920, about 20 million northern Europeans arrived in America. In the 1890s, southern and eastern Europeans joined them. Other immigrants came from the West Indies and Mexico.

Newcomers usually started their life in America in large cities. Most of them lived in neighborhoods with others from their home countries. They didn't know English or how to get jobs. Native-born Americans often discriminated against them and barred them from good jobs.

Poverty

As some Americans grew wealthy, others suffered from poverty. Native Americans on the reservations were very poor. Poverty also was common on farms, in the South, and in big cities.

New farm machinery made larger farms possible. But machines were expensive, and most farmers had to take out high-interest bank loans to buy them. Low crop prices and high shipping costs hurt farmers too.

Poverty was widespread in the South. Cities, towns, and farms had been destroyed in the Civil War. Southern banks failed, and few people had money to invest. State governments passed high taxes to pay for rebuilding. Railroad shipping rates were high. Northerners owned many Southern businesses. However, Southern industries such as forestry, mining, tobacco, furniture-making, and textiles did well.

More poverty could be found in big cities. Among the poor were underpaid workers, immigrants, and African Americans. These groups often lived in slum housing, in crowded and filthy conditions.

Reform Movements

Between 1865 and 1900, reformers tried to bring change. Farmers in the Midwest started the Populist movement. Workers in some industries

▲

Mulberry Street was in New York City's "Little Italy" neighborhood, a new home for thousands of Italian immigrants at the turn of the twentieth century.

formed labor unions. These groups used bargaining and strikes to seek higher wages and better working conditions. The reformer Jacob Riis (rees) exposed problems in New York City's slums. The city made efforts to help. Other movements also tried to aid the urban poor.

In 1848, the women's suffrage movement was organized, seeking equality and voting rights for women. It took until 1920 for the movement to win.

Time Line

1862—Homestead Act encourages western settlement.

1865—Civil War ends.

1866—Ku Klux Klan is founded.

1869—Transcontinental railroad is completed.

1877—Reconstruction ends in the South.

1879—Edison invents the electric light bulb.

1882—Chinese Exclusion Act bars Chinese from entering the United States.

1887—Dawes Act divides tribal lands into individual family farms.

1890—Sioux are massacred at Wounded Knee; Sherman Anti-Trust Act tries to control monopolies; Jacob Riis describes New York slums in *How the Other Half Lives*.

1896—*Plessy* v. *Ferguson* approves "separate but equal" facilities for African Americans.

▲

This photograph shows farm life on the Great Plains.

Reconstruction

Reconstruction and P. B. S. Pinchback

BY JUDITH LLOYD YERO

In the years right after the Civil War, there were great changes in the South. The United States government set rules for how the former Confederate states would be readmitted to the Union. The states had to hold conventions to write new constitutions. Laws were passed to prevent men who had been loyal to the Confederacy from holding political office. Government troops were posted in the South to protect the rights of African Americans.

Things were very unsettled, and this made it easy for wicked men to do their evil deeds. It also made it possible for good things to happen in strange ways.

Portrait of P. B. S. Pinchback.

Onto this scene came a man with the impressive name of **Pinckney Benton Stewart Pinchback**. He was the freeborn son of a Georgia plantation owner, William Pinchback, and a freed slave named Eliza Steward. Pinchback grew up in his father's huge plantation mansion with all the advantages of white children. But his father's white family and friends didn't approve.

When he was nine, Pinchback was sent to school in Ohio to be educated, because black children could not get an education in the pre-Civil War South. Two years later, his beloved father died. Eliza fled to Ohio, fearing that William's white relatives would re-enslave her and the children. Pinchback attended high school in Cincinnati.

To earn money for his family, Pinchback started shining shoes on a Mississippi River steamboat. He made extra money carrying luggage for travelers. He soon noticed that they paid him better if he avoided his well-mannered speech and said "Yes, Massa," as was expected of black people.

People and Terms to Know

Pinckney Benton Stewart Pinchback—(1837–1921) first black governor in the United States.

Pinchback caught the eye of George Devol, a riverboat gambler. Devol taught Pinchback his tricks, and soon they were a team. While Devol cheated the gentlemen in the ship's fancy game room, Pinchback robbed the workers in the lower deck.

Once, when they were forced to run for their lives, Pinchback told Devol he had other plans. "I'm going to do better," Pinchback said. "I'm going to get into that good old legislature, and I'll make Rome howl if I get there." Devol

"I'm going to get into that good old legislature, and I'll make Rome howl if I get there."

probably couldn't imagine a black man in the legislature. But P. B. S. Pinchback wasn't kidding!

When the Civil War started, Pinchback helped the Union cause. He ran a blockade to reach New Orleans. In 1862, he recruited a company of black soldiers for the Union army. He became the company's captain, but the Union army replaced all of his other black officers with whites. In 1863, Pinchback quit in protest.

Pinchback moved to Alabama, where he continued to encourage blacks to demand their rights. "You are equal! Protest against this treatment, against these outrages, and make your voices heard." Blacks in the South were afraid of losing what little ground they'd gained. They privately praised Pinchback but publicly ignored his calls.

In 1867, Pinchback returned to Louisiana. He had his mind set on representing blacks in the new state government. The **Reconstruction** Act of 1867 said that the new Southern state governments had to let African-American men vote. It also said they had to ratify the Fourteenth Amendment, which made it very difficult for men who had been leaders in the Confederacy to hold political office. These things severely weakened the **Democratic Party**. Pinchback met with members of the **Republican Party**. These **scalawags**, whom most white Southerners hated, welcomed African Americans. Pinchback rose quickly in the Republican Party. He served as a delegate to the Constitutional Convention and later as a state senator.

People and Terms to Know

Reconstruction—(1865–1877) process after the Civil War involving readmission of the eleven Confederate states. The term is also used to refer to the period when this was done.

Democratic Party—one of the two major U.S. political parties. It began under Thomas Jefferson but was almost destroyed by arguments over slavery and the Civil War. It revived after 1876 and became the party of the South until very recent times.

Republican Party—one of the two major U.S. political parties. The Republican Party was founded in 1854 to oppose the extension of slavery. Lincoln was the first Republican president.

scalawags—insulting term for Southerners who supported Reconstruction. Some sincerely hoped to reform the South. But others were corrupt and joined the Republican Party for political and financial gain. Scalawags was originally a term for worthless cattle.

As senator, Pinchback, along with other African-American congressmen, proposed a state university for "persons of color."

Pinchback joined with whites to support Republican unity, but he upset people sometimes by speaking out for the rights of blacks. They said that he wanted "too much, too soon." Naturally, he had enemies among Southern Democrats. He also had them within his own party. Louisiana newspapers were filled with lies and exaggerations about him.

During this time, politicians in Louisiana were very corrupt. Money was exchanged for votes. **Carpetbagger** politicians stole from state funds. State officials openly cheated to make sure they had a majority in congressional voting.

In 1871, Henry C. Warmoth was governor of Louisiana. Some have called him the most corrupt governor in Louisiana's history. He was threatened with **impeachment**. Here's what he came up with.

People and Terms to Know

Carpetbagger—insulting term for Northerners who came to the South after the Civil War. Some wanted to help blacks, but others sought financial and political opportunities. Their name came from the cheap suitcases made of carpet in which they carried their things.

impeachment—accusation in a legal proceeding of a public official who is said to have behaved improperly in office.

▲

This cartoon from a Southern newspaper calls Carl Schurz a "carpetbagger."
Schurz was a Northerner who was elected senator in Missouri in 1868.

Warmoth figured that white men would never impeach him if it meant that a black man would automatically become governor. When his black lieutenant governor died, Warmoth had Pinchback named lieutenant governor. He even offered Pinchback a bribe—$50,000 to help turn the state senate against his impeachment.

Warmoth figured wrong. The next day, Pinchback told the senators about the bribe. In December 1872, Warmoth was impeached, and Pinchback became the first black governor in the United States. However, state elections had just taken place, so he remained in the job for only about a month. Then the newly elected governor took office.

Warmoth was impeached, and Pinchback became the first black governor in the United States.

Pinchback had run for the U.S. Congress in that election of 1872 and had won. But the political situation in Louisiana was so unsettled that no one was sure who was supposed to be in power. Pinchback was never seated in Congress. At the age of thirty-five, his political career was over. He continued to serve in only minor roles, including trustee of Southern University at Baton Rouge, the school he had helped establish when he was a legislator.

Pinchback made a success of several business ventures. He and his wife moved to Washington, D.C., and became well known in black society. But when Pinchback died in 1921, the gains he had fought for in the South had faded. The South had become a rigidly segregated society controlled by an all-white Democratic Party.

*　　*　　*

P. B. S. Pinchback was the *only* black governor in United States history until L. Douglas Wilder was elected governor of Virginia in 1989—more than 100 years after Pinchback's short term of office.

QUESTIONS TO CONSIDER

1. What did Pinchback mean when he said, "I'll make Rome howl if I get there"?

2. What did people mean when they suggested that Pinchback wanted "too much, too soon"?

3. Why do you think Pinchback told the senators about Warmoth's bribe? What does this action show about him?

4. What, according to the story, were some of the evil things that happened during Reconstruction?

5. What good things did you read about that happened in strange ways?

Ida B. Wells

BY STEPHEN CURRIE

A jail cell in Memphis, Tennessee
April 3, 1892

Henry Hammond could not stop shivering.

It was long after dinner, and his prison cell was chilly. The floor was hard and cold, and the one moth-eaten blanket was not big enough to cover his whole body. He lay curled on the narrow plank that served as a bed. He hoped that he could somehow get warm and that he would somehow survive the night.

He shivered from the cold.

But mostly, he shivered from fear.

* * *

Photograph of Ida B. Wells.

The offices of the **Memphis _Free Speech_**
April 3, 1892

I leaned on my broom, and I watched **Miss Wells**
at her editor's desk. I watched her write, cross out,
write again. I marveled at a woman who could write
that fast and spell that well. It made me feel proud
for my people, even if it made me feel bad for me.
I didn't know how to read. I couldn't write. But still
I bought her **pink paper** every day. Most of us in the
black community did, even if we had to have our
neighbors or children read it to us. I always asked my
son—my son Henry. I paused in my thoughts.

"You're here late tonight, ma'am," I said softly.

She murmured something about these being
troubling times.

I knew I needed to get back to work. Miss Wells
paid me to clean, not to talk. But my troubles were
heavy on my mind, and I could not sweep them

People and Terms to Know

Memphis _Free Speech_—newspaper edited and partly owned by Ida B.
Wells, aimed at an African-American readership in Memphis, Tennessee,
and surrounding areas of the South.

Miss Wells—Ida B. Wells (1862–1931), newspaper editor who became a
crusader for racial justice. She wrote and spoke out against the frequent
mob killings of African Americans that were going on in the South.

pink paper—The Memphis _Free Speech_ was printed on pink paper so
people who could not read could identify it easily.

away like I could sweep away scraps of paper from around Miss Wells's desk.

"Miss Wells?" I asked, and I gripped my broom tightly. "It's about my son—"

*   *   *

The jail cell
April 3, 1892

Henry Hammond twisted on the narrow plank. His knee and back hurt, and his fear was almost overwhelming. Would this be the last night of his life?

Trust in God, his father had always told him. Pray. All right, Henry said to himself, he would pray. Wincing as he climbed off the plank, he knelt on the cold stone floor and tried to focus his mind.

But all he could think of was what had happened that morning.

His knee and back hurt, and his fear was almost overwhelming.

The day had begun like any other. Henry worked as a delivery-man for Menken's department store in Memphis. The job did not pay well, but it was about all that a young African American could get.

Even a young man with enough education to read the *Free Speech* aloud to his father in the late afternoon could not get a better job.

"B̲e careful," he remembered the white boss telling him this morning. "Things are tense out there. Don't do anything foolish."

"I won't," Henry had promised, and off he'd gone, delivering packages to black customers—hats and shoes, toys and furniture. He'd delivered a few books to the *Free Speech* office, where his father worked as janitor. Everything was normal—until just before noon, when he'd taken a short cut through a white neighborhood.

Foolish, foolish, foolish! he thought, feeling the hard stone cutting into his knees. He should have known better. Blacks in Memphis stayed out of the white neighborhoods whenever they could help it. You never knew what might happen. That's what his father always said. And that was what the lady editor at the *Free Speech* said. And the white boss had been saying it, too, if only Henry had been listening.

Better pray hard, he told himself.

Better pray, because you are going to need all the help you can get.

*   *   *

The offices of the Memphis *Free Speech*
April 3, 1892

"Someone thought he was a burglar," I said. Miss Wells watched me, her face unmoving. "Six white men with sticks and clubs blocked his way. He was frightened, Miss Wells. He's only seventeen. And so he ran."

And they caught him, I added in my head, and beat him up, and the police took him to jail. But I didn't need to say it. That was an old story for us. Miss Wells knew it as well as I did.

Better pray, because you are going to need all the help you can get.

Miss Wells sighed. "Negroes are sent to jail for stealing five cents worth of bread or meat," she said. "Whites are made honored citizens, when they steal thousands."

"And then—" The words stuck in my throat. "And then—a white woman—said—she said she had been attacked by a black man."

▲
Thomas Nast's 1874 cartoon "Worse Than Slavery" shows the threat that white terrorist groups posed to African Americans.

Very slowly, Miss Wells shook her head. Her eyes were full of sympathy.

"Miss Wells—" Terrible things happen to black men who are accused of attacking white women. The thoughts came rushing out before I could stop them. "Miss Wells, will they **lynch** my son?" I imagined Henry, a rope around his neck, being carried to a tree in the dead of the night. "My son is innocent, Miss Wells, he is a good man—"

"They lynched **Tom Moss**," Miss Wells said gently. "He was well liked, a favorite with everyone.

People and Terms to Know

lynch—to put a person to death, usually by hanging, without a lawful trial. Lynching is most often a mob action.

Tom Moss—one of three Memphis men lynched in March 1892; the episode helped spark Ida Wells's anti-lynching work.

He and his wife were the best friends I had. Yet he was murdered with no more consideration than if he had been a dog."

I slumped against the wall. "Then—there's no hope," I whispered.

"There is nothing we can do about lynchings now," Miss Wells told me. "We are outnumbered and without weapons. But the way to right wrongs is to turn the light of truth upon them." She held up a copy of her pink paper, and now I saw fire in her eyes. "This newspaper will keep the waters troubled."

> "The way to right wrongs is to turn the light of truth upon them."

Miss Wells had written much about lynchings. She had made it clear she would neither forgive nor forget the violence of the mob. The whites held the power—we all knew that. The police made no arrests. But we could talk about the lynchings, complain about them, call for justice. We could leave town, perhaps buy weapons of our own. In that way, I saw, there was action. In that way there was hope.

"But what about my son?" The warmth of my tears was on my face. "Is there nothing we can do for him?" I took a breath. "Would you come down to the jail with me so I might see him and give him comfort?" I could not go alone; I doubted they would let me in. But Miss Wells, an editor, a woman—perhaps they would let her see him.

Perhaps she could somehow stop the mob, stop the lynching. In my mind's eye I could see them coming to the prison now, carrying guns, bottles, knives, the rope. . . .

Miss Wells said nothing at all, but stood up and put on her coat.

*   *   *

The jail cell
April 3, 1892

The jail was still and silent. Henry Hammond gazed out at the moon, ignoring the throbbing pain in his side. Would this be the last time he would ever see it?

He remembered what had happened to Tom Moss and the others. He remembered how it had been described in the *Free Speech*. A mob of white men came to the jail. There was a soft knock on the door, late at night. The jailer answered. Men burst in. They opened the cell and seized the prisoner inside. They carried him off to a tree and—

He wished he had not walked through the white neighborhood.

But mostly, he wished that his people could be treated fairly and with respect.

"If I am to die," he murmured, "let people remember my death." Maybe Miss Wells at the *Free Speech* would write about him. Maybe his death—if death was his fate—would help bring about new laws and customs.

Henry Hammond closed his eyes and prayed and listened to the silence.

And then there was a soft knock at the door.

QUESTIONS TO CONSIDER

1. How do you know from the story that African Americans faced racism in Memphis in 1892? What specific lines or passages make that clear?

2. What did Ida B. Wells mean when she said, "The way to right wrongs is to turn the light of truth upon them"?

3. Why do you think mobs took to lynching when the supposed criminals were already in jail?

4. In what ways might Ida B. Wells have been a role model within the African-American community? What evidence in the story supports your answer?

5. Who do you think was knocking on the door at the end of the story? Why?

The Cause of Lynching

In a 1901 magazine article, Ida B. Wells examined the press record to attack the common defense that African Americans were lynched only for serious crimes.

[The record] shows that men, not a few but hundreds, have been lynched for misdemeanors [minor offenses], while others have suffered death for no offense known to the law, the causes assigned being "mistaken identity," "insult," "bad reputation," "unpopularity," "violating contract," "running quarantine," "giving evidence," "frightening child by shooting at rabbits," etc. . . . As only Negroes are lynched for no "offense," "unknown offenses," offenses not criminal, misdemeanors, and crimes not capital, it must be admitted that the real cause of lynching in all such cases is race prejudice, and should be so classified.

Princess of the Press:
The Story of Ida B. Wells-Barnett
by Angela Shelf Medearis

This brief biography is an introduction to the life and career of the pioneer African-American journalist Ida B. Wells.

Ida B. Wells-Barnett:
Crusader Against Lynching
by Elaine Slivinski Lisandrelli

This account of the career of Ida B. Wells emphasizes her courageous anti-lynching campaign.

Ida B. Wells:
Mother of the Civil Rights Movement
by Judith Bloom Fradin and Dennis Brindell Fradin

The Fradins present a detailed record of the career of Ida B. Wells and of the times in which she lived.

In the Land of Jim Crow

BY STEPHEN FEINSTEIN

"Separate but equal really means separate but unequal." That thought kept coming back to me as I traveled through the South in the summer of 1900. I was a journalist for a Chicago newspaper. The publisher, Mr. Richard Holdener, had said to me, "Mr. Martin, it's been four years since _Plessy v. Ferguson_. I want you to spend some time in the South. Talk to people, especially black folk. I want to know what kind of effect this Supreme Court ruling has had on their lives." Most likely Mr. Holdener

---

People and Terms to Know

Plessy v. Ferguson—(1896) U.S. Supreme Court decision that permitted states to set up racially separate public services. This decision wasn't reversed until the 1954 _Brown v. Board of Education_ decision, which outlawed school segregation.

An African American is forced to leave a railroad car.

chose me for this because I'm black. But I was thrilled with the assignment. So off I went.

I was hoping to have good news to report, though it wasn't likely. In *Plessy* v. *Ferguson*, the U.S. Supreme Court had ruled that it was all right for states to set up separate **public facilities** for blacks and whites. Those facilities just had to be "separate but equal."

It had all started with Homer Plessy, a black man in Louisiana. He had tried to ride in a railroad car that was for whites only. He was taken off the car and arrested. Judge John Ferguson gave him a fine and a prison sentence. Plessy took the case to the Supreme Court, complaining that his constitutional rights had been violated. But the highest court in the land ruled otherwise. Justice **John Marshall Harlan** was the only justice who disagreed. He wrote, "Our Constitution is color-blind, and neither knows nor tolerates classes among citizens. In respect of civil rights, all citizens are equal before the law. . . . The thin disguise of equal accommodations

---

People and Terms to Know

public facilities—services such as buses, trains, schools, parks, and swimming pools that are usually available for everyone.

John Marshall Harlan—(1833–1911) U.S. Supreme Court justice.

for passengers in railway coaches will not mislead anyone, nor atone for the wrong this day done."

In fact, I learned that the separate facilities for blacks were rarely equal to those for whites. One day, before boarding the train in New Orleans, I had looked around for a water fountain. It was a hot day, and I was thirsty. I found a clean, carved stone fountain outside the railroad station. As I bent over to take a drink, a voice snarled, "What do you think you're doing, boy?" Startled, I looked around. A white police officer was glaring at me.

A sign above the alley said "FOR COLORED ONLY."

Before I could say a word, he pointed to the entrance to an alley. A sign above the alley said "FOR COLORED ONLY." The "fountain" was a faucet sticking out of a wall. Controlling my anger, I thanked the officer and walked over to the "colored" fountain. As I drank the water, I thought about Homer Plessy being forced off the train car and arrested by a police officer.

I boarded the train, making sure to stay away from the coach for whites. After all, this was the East Louisiana Railway, the very railroad line on which Plessy had been arrested. I took a seat by a window. All the other passengers in my car, as I had expected, were black. The train slowly pulled out of the station, and we soon left New Orleans behind.

All day the train chugged across the farmlands of southern Louisiana. I thought about my experiences so far. I shouldn't have been surprised by the water fountain. After all, I had been turned away from white hotels and restaurants throughout the South. Now we were passing one cotton field after another. Men, women, and children, their backs stooped, were hard at work in the fields, picking cotton. All of them were black like me. And all of them were supposed to be free, like me. I felt as if nothing had changed in thirty-eight years. Back then, people in the fields were slaves, working for the plantation owner. And thirty-eight years ago, as a young boy of eight, I was slaving in the fields with the others. Thirty-eight years ago, I, too, was a slave on a Louisiana cotton plantation.

I closed my eyes. My thoughts drifted back to those days of my youth. It seemed a lifetime ago. Indeed, it was a different life. Since then I had gone from slave to journalist. After the Civil War, all slaves were freed. I went to school. I studied hard and learned to read and write by the time I was twelve. I still worked on the plantation, along with the other former slaves. But I now got paid for my work. And I kept studying and reading.

At sixteen, I left the plantation. I had never known my parents. I had no brothers or sisters. The plantation had been my only home. But after reading all about the world beyond the South, I wanted to see it. I yearned for adventure. I traveled north, living in different cities and working at all kinds of jobs. In Chicago, I got a job running errands at a newspaper. In a stroke of luck, the publisher found out I could write. He gave me a chance to report on some local events. And now he was giving me my big chance.

"You're looking at those sharecroppers like you've never seen a cotton field before."

I opened my eyes and saw yet another cotton farm whizzing by. I wondered about the people working in the fields. Had life really changed for them? Did any of them own that land?

At the next stop, a well-dressed, middle-aged gentleman sat down next to me. As we passed another farm, he said to me, "You're looking at those **sharecroppers** like you've never seen a cotton field before. I'd say you're not from around here."

People and Terms to Know

sharecroppers—tenant farmers who work the land for a share of the crop minus charges. A sharecropper usually is provided with credit for seed, tools, living quarters, and food.

▲

Young African-American sharecroppers pick cotton in Mississippi around 1880.

"On the contrary, sir. I grew up here in Louisiana. I was a plantation slave, and I used to pick cotton as a child. At least those folks out there are no longer slaves," I said. I told the man that I had been living in the North for many years. This was my first trip back to the South.

The man introduced himself as Mr. Lawrence Laval, a businessman who owned clothing shops in New Orleans and Baton Rouge. "Those sharecroppers out there may not be slaves, but they are not free, not by a long shot!" he said. "Many of them are so deeply in debt to the landowners that they can never leave. They would be jailed or whipped if they tried."

When I expressed surprise, Mr. Laval said, "My friend, I'm sorry to say that for every step forward, we take two steps back. The South is now the land of <u>Jim Crow</u>. Too many whites are dead set against racial equality. They are determined to keep us down."

"But what about the Constitution?" I cried. "Every one of us was granted full citizenship."

"True in theory," said Mr. Laval. "But right now it seems like an impossible dream, at least here in the South. Black folk are treated as second-class citizens. Ever since *Plessy* v. *Ferguson*, Southern states pass laws almost every day to keep blacks and whites separate. People call them Jim Crow laws. They stop us from voting, holding public office, serving on juries, living in certain neighborhoods, or marrying a person of another race."

People and Terms to Know

Jim Crow—system of customs and laws that discriminated against African Americans. The name came from a character in minstrel shows, which used a low form of humor to stereotype blacks.

He paused and glanced out the window. "Here in Louisiana, black voters have dropped from about 130,000 to little more than 1,000! Voters now must take **literacy tests**. White voting registrars make sure that even educated black men do not pass. And we have to pay a **poll tax** that most poor folk cannot afford."

"Here in Louisiana, black voters have dropped from about 130,000 to little more than 1,000!"

"'Separate but equal' has been used to justify—," I started.

"Separate but equal really means separate but unequal!" Mr. Laval interrupted, impatiently. "There now are separate schools, hospitals, parks, restaurants, theaters, stores, and restrooms. In most cases, the facilities and services for blacks are of much lower quality than those for whites."

The more I heard, the more angry and upset I became. The signs of progress I had been hoping to

---

People and Terms to Know

literacy tests—tests that determine whether a person can read and write. The requirement of literacy tests for voters was a way around the Fifteenth Amendment. It kept many African Americans from voting.

poll tax—tax that had to be paid before voting. Poll taxes were commonly used in the South to prevent blacks and poor whites from voting. They were outlawed by the Constitution's Twenty-fourth Amendment (1964).

report did not exist in the South. Outside the train window, the sun was sinking in the west. Shadows of fieldworkers were lengthening across the cotton fields. Was there any hope at all for them? My heart was filled with sorrow.

I decided then and there to write the full truth about the Jim Crow laws. I wanted readers to become as outraged as I was. People should learn that here in America citizens were being denied their constitutional rights. Maybe things would change for the better someday.

*   *   *

It was not until the Civil Rights movement of the 1960s, however, that the "someday" Mr. Martin dreamed of came about. Discrimination had been practiced openly, and with the help of laws, for one hundred years after the Civil War.

QUESTIONS TO CONSIDER

1. What did Justice Harlan mean when he wrote, "Our Constitution is color-blind"?

2. Why did Mr. Martin leave the South when he was a young man of sixteen?

3. What was Mr. Martin's reaction to seeing the fieldworkers picking cotton?

4. What did Mr. Laval mean when he said, "Separate but equal really means separate but unequal"?

"What a Colored Man Should Do To Vote"

A pamphlet published in Philadelphia some-time between 1900 and 1910 advised African Americans about voting laws in the South:

In Alabama, Louisiana, Mississippi, North Carolina, South Carolina, Virginia, and Tennessee

You must pay your poll tax.

You must register and hold certificate of registration.

If you can read and write you can register.

In Alabama, Louisiana, and South Carolina

If you cannot read and write you can register if you own $300 worth of property.

In Arkansas and Georgia

You must pay your poll tax.

In Florida, Kentucky, Texas, and West Virginia

You must reside in the state.

A man convicted of almost any crime may be barred from voting.

part two

The Immigrants

Gold Mountain

BY DIANE WILDE

Seventeen-year-old Foon Lee sat behind the counter in his Uncle Chang's herb and medicine shop. He looked around the small dark room. He was new at this. He wasn't sure how to use all of the Chinese herbs and teas. Uncle Chang knew how to use every one of them to cure illnesses and help people stay healthy.

In San Francisco's growing **Chinatown**, every-one respected his uncle and relied on his skill in traditional Chinese medicine. A few weeks ago, Uncle Chang had chosen Foon Lee to learn the

---

People and Terms to Know

Chinatown—neighborhood or section of a city that is inhabited mostly by Chinese people.

San Francisco's Chinatown in 1898.

business and work with him. Foon Lee felt both honored and grateful. Perhaps now his future would be secure!

Foon Lee thought about how awful he'd felt nine years ago, in 1873, when he'd arrived in this city. For six weeks, he and his father had been at sea, traveling from China to this new land. Like others in their hometown, they had called California _Gum San_, the Gold Mountain. They were sure that they would find wealth and acceptance right away.

They called California **Gum San,** _the Gold Mountain._

How stupid they were! As they approached port, they had learned a frightening lesson. A big, angry crowd of people stood on the dock. They yelled and shook their fists saying, "Chinese go home!" and "No more Chinese!"

Foon Lee was only eight at the time. He didn't understand why people were so angry. But Uncle Chang knew. He had arrived in 1852, in the early years of the **gold rush**. Thousands of Chinese

---

People and Terms to Know

Gum San—name, meaning "Gold Mountain," that Chinese people from the Canton area of China gave to California and other areas of the western part of North America where gold was being mined.

gold rush—rapid movement of migrants to an area where gold has been discovered. California's gold rush began in 1848, when gold was discovered at Sutter's Mill. Within a year, about 80,000 miners had flooded into the area from all over the world.

immigrants came during those years. Uncle Chang first had tried working in the mines, sending whatever money he could back to his family in China. But **discrimination** against Chinese forced him out of the gold fields.

Chinese often were driven out of jobs, Uncle Chang had said. Many white people feared the Chinese because they looked, talked, and acted so differently. Also, Chinese people worked very hard, and for lower wages than were paid to white people. So white workers feared they would lose their jobs because bosses could get the work done more cheaply by hiring Chinese.

Uncle Chang went back to San Francisco. Luckily, he knew a trade that the Chinese people needed and respected. He opened his medicine shop in San Francisco. Soon he was making a good living.

People and Terms to Know

discrimination—unfair treatment of a person or group based on negative ideas about such characteristics as skin color, nationality, religion, or gender.

Uncle Chang had helped Foon Lee and his father after they arrived. Foon Lee's father found work on the railroad, where many other Chinese worked. He worked and he saved, even though he was hardly paid enough to keep them alive. Finally, he had saved enough money to bring Foon Lee's mother from China. For the next several years, the family was together, though they had to move often for his father to be near his work. When Foon Lee was twelve, his father died in a railroad accident. Then Uncle Chang brought Foon Lee and his mother back to Chinatown to live near him.

> *He worked and he saved, even though he was hardly paid enough to keep them alive.*

Foon Lee looked at the clock. Where was Min Yee? He looked forward to seeing her every day. He always felt on edge when she arrived late for afternoon tea.

He began to worry. Things were very tough for Chinese people. Earlier this year, the **Chinese Exclusion Act** had been passed. Now it was illegal for Chinese immigrants to enter America. Angry mobs of white people sometimes came to

People and Terms to Know

Chinese Exclusion Act—(1882) federal law that banned all Chinese except students, teachers, merchants, tourists, and government officials from entering the United States. It was the only law ever passed in America that excluded a specific national group. It remained in effect until 1943.

▲

Anti-Chinese feeling was so strong that street riots against the Chinese were not uncommon.

Chinatown to frighten people and even to beat them. Foon Lee especially worried about Min Yee's father, who owned a successful fish market. He used his profits to bring relatives from China to San Francisco. Some white people knew about this. It was dangerous!

Foon Lee knew that Min Yee's uncle was scheduled to arrive from Canton tonight. In all the excitement, perhaps Min Yee didn't have time for tea today. Still, Foon Lee would miss her smiling face coming through the door.

The afternoon wore on. Foon Lee followed his uncle's orders, mixing medicines, teas, and broths for customers. Suddenly the door to the shop flew open. Min Yee's brother raced into the room, out of breath. The look on his face told Foon Lee that something was very wrong. Uncle Chang also saw it. As quickly as he could, Uncle Chang finished giving a customer ailanthus seeds, a remedy for her arthritis, and then closed the door behind her.

"What has happened?" Uncle Chang asked.

"Our family has been threatened!" Min Yee's brother said. "This morning, a tall white man came to the market. He grabbed Min Yee's arm and gave her a warning for father. 'We know,' the man said, 'about the delivery at the dock tonight. If we see a new package hanging around the market, we'll have a special welcome for him. No one will ever forget it!'"

Min Yee's brother appealed to Uncle Chang. "My father and sister are afraid for our market and for our uncle arriving tonight. We don't know what to do. We can't meet the boat, and we can't have him in the market. These white men watch us, and they will know. Other stores already have been attacked."

Foon Lee felt anger building up inside him. How could this man treat Min Yee so roughly and

"Our family has been threatened!" Min Yee's brother said.

threaten her family! Foon Lee wanted to run to the market to protect them. But he knew he should wait for Uncle Chang to speak.

For a long time, Uncle Chang frowned and was silent. Then he sighed deeply and said, "It pains me to find such hatred around us. But we can help you."

Uncle Chang looked at Foon Lee. "Go down to the dock while it is still light. Find the white man, Mr. Kelley, who runs the shipping office. He is a friend. Over the years, he has handled many shipments of herbs from China for me. When his son was very ill with a fever, I helped him. He will help us now.

"Tell your family to act normally. Do everything that you always do."

"Give Mr. Kelley the name of the uncle, the name of the ship, and the time it is expected to dock. Tell him to send someone to meet the boat. He can hide the uncle in his closet until I arrive. After dark, I will bring the uncle back here. He can stay in our treatment room until it's safe for him to go outside."

Uncle Chang turned to Min Yee's brother. "Tell your family to act normally. Do everything that you always do. Close the shop at the usual time. Go to bed early. I will send Foon Lee to visit Min Yee in the morning with news.

"Everyone is getting used to seeing Foon Lee visit your sister." Uncle Chang smiled at Foon Lee. Then again to Min Yee's brother he said, "Now go! Tell your family not to worry. It is a good thing to have friends who owe favors."

Foon Lee hurried into his hat and coat to leave for the dock. As he put his hand on the doorknob, his uncle stopped him. "You are learning well, Foon Lee, in many ways. This is a time to be calm. Do just what you have been asked to do. Don't let your feelings drive you. You will find the courage to act with certainty. Then return immediately. Be back before nightfall."

Foon Lee took a deep breath and set out. His uncle had been right. Mr. Kelley had quickly nodded his head at the request. He would take care of it. Foon Lee left the docks and climbed the hills in the thickening fog. He arrived back in Chinatown at dusk.

At 10 P.M., Uncle Chang left the house, quietly. Much later, he returned. With him was Min Yee's uncle, exhausted and frightened. Foon Lee was waiting for them with hot tea and soup. The three of them ate and drank and talked together softly. The uncle spoke of the hardships he had left behind him in China. "Life in America is much better," Uncle Chang told him. "Difficult, yes, but much better."

In the morning, Foon Lee left for the fish market with a light heart and a feeling of pride. He didn't know when the hatred between the Chinese and their white neighbors would end. He hoped that his children would not have to live in fear this way. But he was glad to be on his way to tell Min Yee that her uncle was safely asleep in Uncle Chang's shop. Foon Lee felt proud that he and his uncle had helped her family. His reward would be the special smile that he knew was always saved for him.

QUESTIONS TO CONSIDER

1. What dangers and obstacles did Chinese immigrants face in California during and after the gold rush? Why?

2. What does Uncle Chang mean when he says, "It is a good thing to have friends who owe favors"?

3. In what ways do you think that living in Chinatowns might have helped Chinese immigrants?

4. In what ways might the existence of Chinatowns have contributed to a climate of prejudice?

5. Why do you think that Foon Lee and his family didn't turn to the police to help them?

6. Why do you think Chinese immigrants came to America, considering the prejudice they faced?

Anti-Chinese Prejudice

In a magazine article written in 1903, a Chinese immigrant explained how prejudice limited Chinese opportunity in America:

The reason why so many Chinese go into the laundry business is because it requires little capital and is one of the few opportunities that are open. Men of other nationalities who are jealous of the Chinese, because he is a more faithful worker than one of their people, have raised such an outcry about Chinese cheap labor that they have shut him out of working on farms or in factories or building railroads or making streets or digging sewers. He cannot practice any trade, and his opportunities to do business are limited to his own countrymen. So he opens a laundry when he quits domestic service.

Journey to Gold Mountain:
The Chinese in 19th-century America
by Ronald T. Takaki

Chinese immigrants saw the United States as "Gold Mountain." When they reached America, they usually found hardship and prejudice. Ronald T. Takaki describes their experiences.

The Journal of Wong Ming-Chung:
A Chinese Miner
by Laurence Yep

This historical novel by award-winning writer Laurence Yep describes the adventures of an eleven-year-old Chinese boy who leaves his home to come to America during the California gold rush.

The Chinese American Family Album
by Dorothy and Thomas Hoobler

The Hooblers use photographs, letters, journals, oral histories, and newspaper accounts to present the Chinese-American experience.

Traveling Steerage

BY DEE MASTERS

In 1890, we lived in a one-room mud hut with an earthen floor in the Pale, the region in Russia where Jews were permitted to live. My father was the only one in our village who could read. He studied the **Torah**, the holy learning of the Jewish people.

One day, all the children of our Jewish village had gathered in our hut. Our speckled hen and her chicks pecked at the potato peelings that mother dropped as she fixed our noon meal. My father was teaching these village children, even though it was against the law. The law said, "No chadir [Hebrew school] shall be held in a room used for cooking

---

People and Terms to Know

Torah—body of Jewish law and tradition; also, the first five books of the Hebrew Bible.

European immigrants crowd the deck of a ship arriving in New York in 1902.

and sleeping." But we couldn't go to the town school. It was for Christians only.

Mother put the cooked potatoes and black bread on the table. All of us rushed to get our share. And, while we ate, we were caught. The door was kicked down! A **Cossack** rushed in! A whip cracked! The children ran screaming out of the house. My mother wailed, and my father stood, grief stricken.

While we ate, we were caught.
The door was kicked down! A Cossack rushed in!

"A thousand **rubles** fine or a year in prison if you are ever found again teaching children where you're eating or sleeping," shouted the Cossack. How could we live without what my father made from his teaching? But, of course, the **czar** did not wish us to live.

As I watched the Cossack go off, a crowd appeared. Almost everyone in the village came! More trouble? No, Masheh Mindel, the water

---

People and Terms to Know

Cossack—warrior peasant from the Ukraine region of Russia. Cossacks were used by the Russian government as police.

rubles—units of Russian money.

czar (zahr)—ruler of Russia. This Russian word is from the Latin word *caesar*, meaning "emperor."

---

carrier's wife, had received a letter from her husband in America. She needed my father to read it.

Gedalyeh Mindel, the water carrier, wrote that he had a business, a pushcart, selling fruit. He made at least two dollars profit each day, four rubles! Masheh Mindel had a successful husband in America! He wrote that he ate white bread and meat every day. People called him "Mister." There were no mud huts in America. He had a separate room with a door. There was no czar in America! No czar! And finally, he was sending his wife fifty rubles to come to America.

I almost hated them. Why couldn't we go? Isn't every heart hungry for America? Everyone wanted to go to America. How could we get there?

"The czar is pushing us to America," my mother laughed.

"What—where—America? With what money?" answered my father, his face full of fear and sorrow.

We could sell everything, everything we owned. We would be happy in America. We decided to do it. We piled everything we owned into one big pile in the middle of the hut. Then we called the money lender. We needed one hundred rubles to get to America.

"I will give you thirty," he said. But, in the end, my mother got a hundred rubles from him. We would go **steerage**, no better than cattle, but what did we care? We would eat white bread and meat every day in America! We could say what we believed, and no Cossack would whip us. Christians and Jews are like brothers in America! No fear in America. Nobody is better than another in America. Everybody could go to school in America, free school. Where I was born I was a stranger, but in America I would be welcomed.

Where I was born I was a stranger, but in America I would be welcomed.

Most of the village came with us to the train when we left. Women wept. "How will you deal with the police?" "Tickets?" "The sea?" "Don't forget. . . ." "Take care. . . . " "God help you!" "Remember!"

Great puffs of steam rose from the engine. The train whistle blew! The train took us away from where we had lived all our lives, forever.

People and Terms to Know

steerage—part of a passenger ship occupied by those traveling at the cheapest rate.

We had only a little money, our tickets, and our passports to help us travel 5,000 miles and cross an ocean. We did not get far. German doctors stopped us at the border. There was **cholera**. We could only continue if we had two hundred rubles more than we had. They took our identification papers. My mother cried and begged a German guard for help. He sent us to Herr Schidorsky, whose brother was chairman of an **emigrant** aid association. (After all these years, we still pray for those two men.) We stayed at his house until we were allowed to continue.

We were put in railway cars. At every stop, more and more emigrants were pushed into the cars. All we knew were trains—depots—crowds—heat—crowds—trains. Everything went faster and faster. Where were we? Where were we going? At several stops, our bundles were taken away from us and steamed, to kill any disease we might carry. We had to rub strange, bad smelling oil on our bodies. What was this? We were showered without warning!

"Quick! Quick, or you will miss the train!"

People and Terms to Know

cholera—deadly infectious disease whose outbreaks often spread out of control.

emigrant—one who leaves a country. An immigrant is one who enters a country.

After the train, we were taken we-knew-not-where by horse carts. Always people wanted more money. The last place was a prison. There we were **quarantined** for two weeks, several hundred of us, all behind bars and high walls. We could hear the ocean but could not see it. Finally, we were loaded onto the deck of a ship and were on the water. We were really on our way!

We were on that great water for sixteen days.

When would we be in America?

"When you see the **Statue of Liberty**, the big lady!"

We were on that great water for sixteen days. The ship pitched and rolled. Everyone was seasick. Some spent the entire trip throwing up. Men, women, and children were crammed into steerage—the lowest levels in the ship—tight, damp, airless. Bunks rose up in piles. Each passenger had only the space of a bunk. It held bed, clothes and towel rack, cupboard, and baggage space. There was no place to put trash, no place if you got seasick. In steerage, there was a constant smell of sickness.

People and Terms to Know

quarantined—put into isolation for a period of time to prevent disease from spreading.

Statue of Liberty—giant statue of a woman holding a torch that stands in New York Harbor. Unveiled in 1886, it became a beacon of hope for immigrants.

There was one washroom, used by everyone. It was about seven feet by nine feet. The washbasins had only cold salt water. You washed in them, got sick in them, did laundry in them. Many people did not bathe for the entire trip. If you could imagine how bad it was in steerage for us, you would think we were very unhappy. Many were. But remember where we had come from and where we were going.

We often sailed slowly through dense fog. The sailors knew the route. They slept and ate. But we who had never been on the sea were almost constantly afraid. We felt that the ship would go down, and we would die.

I, like many others, tried to spend most of my time out on the deck, where the air was fresh. Even when it was cold, many of us would wrap in blankets and even sleep on the deck. I explored as much of the ship as I could. The ship's crew was very friendly to me. I mostly remember the sea itself. It was so great, so powerful. The waves were always changing shape. Sometimes when I was on deck, it seemed that there was only me, the sea, and the sky. I loved the ocean. It became a part of me.

"Land! Land!"

"America! America!"

I saw the big lady up ahead, standing on an island, raising her torch!

Everyone rushed up from below, crowding to the rails of the ship. They lifted children to see their new country. Some fell to their knees and prayed. Everyone was crying, laughing, hugging each other. People danced in circles on the deck.

We'd found freedom!

It, of course, was not what we expected, but it was America.

QUESTIONS TO CONSIDER

1. Why was the narrator's family treated so badly in their homeland?

2. How did the people in the narrator's village picture America?

3. What did Gedalyeh Mindel mean when he wrote in his letter that there was no czar in America?

4. Why did people keep asking the narrator's family for money?

5. What would have been the worst part of this trip for you?

A Day at Ellis Island

BY STEPHEN CURRIE

"Get in line, children," murmured Mama. "Have you got the bags, Hans? Liese, hold my hand. Do *not* scratch at your eyes. Good girl. Ida, take the baby."

I took Hilde, my two-year-old sister. She wiggled and shrieked. I felt like wiggling and shrieking too. Hot, sweaty people pressed against me. The air scarcely moved, and it smelled of people who had been at sea for too many days. I was hungry, tired— and nervous.

Here we were at **Ellis Island**, the gateway to America.

People and Terms to Know

Ellis Island—island in New York Harbor used at the turn of the twentieth century for the processing of immigrants to the United States. About 17 million people came through the Great Hall at Ellis Island between 1892 and 1924, most of them before 1914.

Immigrants spent hours, or even days, at Ellis Island, awaiting examination by officials.

Here we were, just a few feet away from a better life.

I *hoped*.

Mama looked back to Liese. "Your *eyes*, darling," she said. "Keep your hands away from your eyes."

Somewhere ahead of us, Papa was waiting. Papa had left our home in **Austria** a year and a half ago. There was no work, and Papa knew that he could get a job in America that would pay him well. So he had gone . . . and now, at last, he had saved enough money to send for us. Papa, Mama, Hans, Liese, the baby Hilde, and me—the whole family would start a new life in America, our new home.

I could not wait to see Papa. I remembered so much about him. I remembered the old black overcoat he always wore in winter. I remembered the way his face burst into a smile, like fireworks, when he was happy. I remembered the smell of peppermint candy when he bought us children a little treat. I remembered the bushy mustache he always wore.

People and Terms to Know

Austria—country in south central Europe that borders Switzerland, Germany, the Czech Republic, Slovakia, Hungary, Slovenia, and Italy. Its people speak German.

Somewhere ahead he was waiting for us—Papa, and his smile, his mustache, and maybe a little candy. But he wouldn't be wearing the overcoat, not in this heat.

People chattered in a dozen different tongues. I heard Italian, Hungarian, Russian, and German, our own language.

I switched the baby to the other arm. Hilde's howls echoed in the large inspection hall and mixed with other noises. People chattered in a dozen different tongues. I heard Italian, Hungarian, Russian, and German, our own language. Now that we were practically Americans, Mama, Hans, and I were speaking English as much as we could.

Liese looked up. *"Mama, Meine Augen tun weh."*

Meine Augen tun weh. "My eyes hurt," I translated to myself. I knew it just from looking at Liese's face. But I had hoped it was not true. There was a sinking feeling deep in my stomach.

"Don't rub them!" Hans's voice was shrill and angry. "You've been rubbing them. Mama told you not to rub them!"

Liese burst into tears.

"Hans. Leave the child alone." Mama spoke softly but firmly. She gathered Liese into the folds of her skirt. "Crying will only make it worse, you know."

Hans bit his lip so hard I could almost see blood. "But if her eyes hurt—" he began.

"We know what might happen," Mama said calmly. "And we hope it does not. But what happens, happens." She stroked Liese's dark hair. "*Weine nicht, Maeuschen klein.*" ("Don't cry, my little mouse.")

Hans stared wildly at me. He was always one to show his fears, while I kept mine to myself. His hands gripped and released the bags, gripped and released. Liese stopped crying. She burrowed deeper into Mama's skirt.

Before we could see Papa, we had to pass inspection. Not all immigrants would be allowed into the United States, Papa had told us in his letters. People who were enemies of the government would be stopped at inspection. Those who were feeble-minded would be stopped.

And those with certain diseases would be stopped too. Papa had said the inspectors would start watching us when we climbed the stairs to the inspection hall. Who limped? Who needed help? Later, they would look more closely. Who had problems of the scalp, the muscles, the heart? Those with serious problems were held and not allowed to enter for a day or a week.

Some people were shipped back home. I could not imagine being sent back to Austria. We had sold everything. We could not make another trip across the sea. Poor Liese had been crying for the last three days. She hated the heat, the rotten smells aboard

▲

Physical examinations at Ellis Island included a test for trachoma, an eye disease common in southern and eastern Europe under conditions of poverty, overcrowding, or poor sanitation.

the ship, and the violent shaking of the ship as it rolled from side to side.

Most of all, we could not go without seeing Papa. But if Liese were sent home, we would have no choice.

"She has been crying from the seasickness," Hans said to Mama. "It is no disease. They cannot keep her out—*us* out—just because her eyes are red and sore."

Mama said nothing. I may have been younger than Hans, but I knew that they could, if they chose to.

One by one, he inspected us— our faces, our throats, our feet.

"Next!" The inspector waved his hand to us. Quickly we moved forward, as if we were afraid he might change his mind. And, one by one, he inspected us—our faces, our throats, our feet. "Take off your hat," he told Hans. He checked his hair for **lice**. "Take off your collar," he told Mama. He checked her neck for sores. "Put that baby down," he told me. He made Hilde walk, and then checked the skin on my arms.

People and Terms to Know

lice—small, wingless insects that enter the hair or skin of people and animals and suck their blood. Their bites can cause itching, redness, and soreness. They spread very easily under the conditions of overcrowding and lack of sanitary facilities found in the steerage of ships. Lice can carry disease, and their bites can lead to infections.

Then he turned to Liese.

I held my breath, hoping he would not notice her eyes. How could he not notice the bitter redness, the sore spots from rubbing them over the last three days? Do not look in her eyes, I whispered to myself.

"Turn and show me your eyes, little one," said the man.

Mama translated into German, keeping the desperation out of her voice. Slowly, Liese turned to the man and looked straight at him. He took a metal stick and pushed up her eyelid. Her watery brown eyes, teary, with angry red lines across the white parts, stared at him.

Behind me, Hans groaned. And, I swear, I did not breathe.

"Hmm," said the man. He moved his lower lip in and out. "How was the crossing for this little girl?"

"Bad," Hans and I said in the same moment.

"Very bad?" asked the man. "Did she have trouble sleeping, trouble eating? Was she rubbing her eyes all the time?"

I did not dare hope. "Yes," I said simply.

Hans echoed me, "Yes."

Mama took a deep breath. "All she needs, sir, is a little rest on dry land and a good hot meal. I promise you, sir, her eyes will be fine. She has no disease, sir, only they hurt, and she rubs them."

"It happens," the man said gently. "We see children with eyes like this nearly every day. You are right. I see no disease. All she needs is rest and food and the trouble goes away. Is there a place you can rest here in New York? Are you meeting someone here after I let you go through?"

"Yes," Mama began, "my husband will meet us—"

But I did not hear the rest of what she had to say. We had passed! I wanted to shout for joy, but my body felt too numb. In a few more minutes, I knew, I would see Papa again, my own Papa. I reached down instead and folded Liese into my own skirt.

"We are home, *Maeuschen*," I whispered happily. "We are home."

QUESTIONS TO CONSIDER

1. Why did Papa go to America? Why do you think that the rest of the family did not accompany him at first?

2. What were some of the reasons that an immigrant might be sent home? Why do you think that the United States had these rules?

3. In what ways would the experience of immigrating to the United States be different today from that of the family in the story?

4. What do you think the immigration policy should be for people who have medical problems? Why?

Ellis Island

In an account of a 1906 visit to Ellis Island, English writer H. G. Wells described the endless stream of immigrants slowly passing through the great central hall:

All day long, through an intricate series of metal pens, the long procession files, step by step, bearing bundles and trunks and boxes, past this examiner and that, past the quick, alert medical officers, the talleymen and the clerks. At every point immigrants are being picked out and set aside for further medical examination, for further questions, for the busy little courts; but the main procession satisfies conditions, passes on. It is a daily procession that, with a yard of space to each, would stretch over three miles. . . . On they go, from this pen to that, pen by pen, towards a desk at a little metal wicket—the gate of America.

Breaker Boys

BY DIANE WILDE

Michael McHugh was awakened by the cold, shrill sound of the mine whistle. He pulled the covers over his head to escape from the chilly morning air. It was 5:30 A.M. Michael knew that this morning he couldn't roll over and go back to sleep, as his younger sisters did. He had to get up and begin his first day of work at the coal mine.

"Michael," his mother shouted. "It's time to get going! Get dressed and come eat."

Michael had just turned nine years old. Today, he would work at the **colliery** for the first time, as a

---

People and Terms to Know

colliery—coal mine and its plant and outbuildings.

Reformer Lewis Hine photographed these boys who mined coal in West Virginia around 1900.

breaker boy. His brother Frank also had started as a breaker boy when he was nine. The law said breaker boys should be twelve, but Father had lied about their ages. Now Frank was fourteen and worked in the mine with Father and the other men.

Michael quickly got dressed for work. Soon he would be making 70 cents per day. He'd come home on payday and put his earnings down on the table, just as Father and Frank did.

He had already visited the huge, gloomy building where the breaker boys sorted broken pieces of coal, rocks, and slate. The boys' job was to separate coal from the unusable rocks. Michael knew that Frank used to get very tired working in the breaker room. It was dangerous work too. Two years ago, Frank's friend Carlo fell into some machinery and was killed.

Michael ate a quick breakfast of thick oatmeal. His mother smiled at him and handed him his tin lunch pail. Then he set off through the snowy darkness with Frank and Father. When they arrived at the breaker building, Michael said good-bye and opened the door.

People and Terms to Know

breaker boy—boy who worked in the breaker building near the coal mine, separating coal chunks from pieces of slate and rock.

Inside the breaker building was a large, noisy room with high walls. Long iron chutes ran at an angle from the top of the breaker near the ceiling on one side of the room to the floor on the far side. Every four or five feet, a pine board, used as a bench, was placed across the chutes. The breaker boys took their places on these benches facing the tops of the chutes.

The breaker boss saw Michael standing inside the entrance. He told Michael to sit next to another boy toward the top of the chute. Michael climbed the narrow flight of steps past coal-blackened wooden beams and grimy windows. As he approached the bench, he was glad to see that he would be sitting next to his friend Johnny.

"Hi, Michael," Johnny shouted. "I'm glad to see you!" Johnny showed Michael how to tie a handkerchief over his nose and mouth. This was to keep them from breathing in the coal dust, steam, and smoke that filled the air as the coal was dumped down the chutes. Johnny also gave Michael a piece of chewing tobacco. This was supposed to prevent the breaker dust from going down his throat.

When the breaker was turned on, the noise made it impossible to talk. The deafening machinery crushed and separated tons of coal into various sizes. As the coal ran down the chute, the boys used their feet to stop the flow. Michael tried to work as fast as he could. He clumsily sorted through and separated the coal with his hands. Johnny showed him how to pick out the slate and rocks and place them in a different chute. Then they lifted their feet, and the coal flowed down to the boys below. The slate and rocks fell into large cars parked at the bottom. When the cars were full, men hauled them away and dumped the rejected rocks, called **culm**, down the side of the hill.

The deafening machinery crushed and separated tons of coal into various sizes. As the coal ran down the chute, the boys used their feet to stop the flow.

The rough, sharp rocks and coal soon made Michael's hands crack and bleed. But gloves weren't allowed, Johnny said. With gloves on, the

---

People and Terms to Know

culm—bits of slate and other rocks that were separated from the coal and discarded. Up to ten million tons of culm were dumped from one breaker in a year, and breaker boys sorted all of it.

boys didn't work as well. Johnny's hands had tough calluses. Michael knew calluses would be slow in coming. He had seen his brother Frank tending his sore and swollen hands every night for weeks.

Out of the corner of his eye, Michael saw the breaker boss wandering among the boys. If anyone fell asleep or worked too slowly, he got smacked on the back of the hands with a stick. Some boys threw rocks at the boss when his back was turned.

▲
These young Pennsylvania coal miners were photographed in 1889.

Over time, Michael got used to the work. Three months into the job, by December, his hands had toughened, and he could work quickly and with skill. But it was hard to get up in the dark, cold mornings and go to work. He felt very tired. His back was sore night and day, from leaning over the chute. Michael was happy to pick up his pay each month, however. And he liked to play ball with the other boys during their lunchtime.

Michael tried to work carefully, knowing that he could get hurt if he didn't. Still, one day, Michael's sleeve got caught in a conveyer belt, and he nearly lost his hand. Johnny saw the machine catch Michael's sleeve and had grabbed Michael, yanking him away from the belt. Michael's jacket sleeve ripped off and went flapping down to the boys below—but he still had his hand! That day, Michael thanked Johnny over and over again.

One frosty day in January, Michael and Johnny heard the emergency whistle blow. That was a signal that there had been an accident in the mine. All of the boys ran out of the breaker building to see what had happened. They saw their mothers running up all the streets of the village, toward the mines.

"What happened?" Michael shouted when he saw his mother.

"One of the tunnels has caved in!" she cried. "Oh, I hope your father and Frank are safe!"

They waited near the mine shaft with the anxious crowd. Finally, they saw Frank emerge from the dust at the entrance to the mine. But Michael's father was not with him. At first, Frank was coughing so much that he could hardly speak. Finally, he choked out the words: "Father was trapped in the cave-in."

"One of the tunnels has caved in!" she cried.

As Frank told the story, people in the waiting crowd began to wail and cry. Frank said that an explosion had trapped three men, including Father, under rock and heavy timbers. The other miners were scrambling to get them out. Then another explosion buried them all for good. Their cries for help had stopped, and the other miners had to give up the rescue because of the danger.

Michael felt like a tree had been uprooted in his chest. How could Father be gone? What would they do now? He broke into heavy sobs.

Then he turned to his mother. She was kneeling on the ground, sobbing quietly into her apron. Frank had sunk down beside her and held her hand. Michael joined them.

"Mother, don't worry," Michael whispered. "We'll be all right. Frank and I will take care of you and the girls. It won't be long before I can join Frank, in the mine."

QUESTIONS TO CONSIDER

1. Why do you think that Michael and his brother went to work as breaker boys?

2. What aspects of becoming a breaker boy did Michael look forward to? In his place, how would you have felt about going to work?

3. As Michael got used to the job, what aspects of being a breaker boy turned out to be difficult?

4. What were some of the hidden dangers of working as a breaker boy or a coal miner?

5. In what ways might changes in the law have helped mine workers and their families of this time?

6. How would you describe the life that Michael and Frank will face as they become men and support their whole family?

A Coal Miner's Bride:
The Diary of Anetka Kaminska
by Susan Campbell Bartoletti

Susan Campbell Bartoletti's historical novel presents the experiences of a 13-year-old girl who leaves her village in Poland for an arranged marriage with a coal miner in Pennsylvania.

Growing Up in Coal Country
by Susan Campbell Bartoletti

Here, Bartoletti describes the harsh lives of children who worked in the coal mines of Pennsylvania 100 years ago, when child labor laws were unknown.

Kids at Work: Lewis Hine and the
Crusade Against Child Labor
by Russell Freedman

The famous photographer Lewis Hine used his camera in a campaign to expose the working conditions of children. In this biography, award-winning writer Russell Freedman presents Hine's life and work.

My Day in the Sweatshop

BY MARIANNE McCOMB

Every day I wake my girls at 6:00. There's just two of 'em now that my eldest, Fanny, is dead from the fever. Patrick, he gets up at 5:00 since he has to be at the factory at 5:30. He's a roller at the cigar factory. The rollers start earlier than the **shirtwaist** girls, which is what me, Emily, and little Mary are.

The girls and I, we work at a factory on the eighth floor of the Asch Building in New York City. It's called the Triangle Shirtwaist Company, but some of the girls call it a **sweatshop**. Patrick says we're lucky enough to have the work since so many

---

People and Terms to Know

shirtwaist—woman's or girl's blouse that usually has a collar and cuffs.

sweatshop—name for a place where workers are employed at low pay for long hours under bad conditions.

Women do tedious piecework in a New York hat factory around 1900.

others have nothing. Emily and I do **piecework**. We have to be at work at 6:30. Little Mary, who's six, starts at 7:00. The three of us walk to work together so I can keep an eye on the girls. Emily and I go in first, and Mary waits outside.

At 6:30 the boss opens the door. I say good-bye to Mary and go right to my sewing machine. My job is to sew the collars on the shirtwaists. The work ain't hard, but it's hurry, hurry, hurry all day long. Sometimes my foot gets sore from running the foot pedal to my machine. First I stitch by hand the inside of the collar on the shirt. Then I quick flip it over and use my machine to sew on the outer edge of the collar. The stitches have to be perfect. If they ain't, I rip 'em out and start again. Ripping out stitches means wasted time, and that means less money for me and the girls. So I'm careful.

Yesterday I got my finger caught in the machine, and the needle went through it three times before I could get my foot to stop pumping

People and Terms to Know

piecework—work that is paid for by the amount of work done, not by the time it takes.

the pedal. My finger bled on a collar. It was ruined, and I had to call the boss over. He called me a stupid fool and worse names and said he'll charge me for that collar. That means a smaller wage this week. I make around $8.00 per week, and Emily makes a little less.

He called me a stupid fool and worse names and said he'll charge me for that collar.

The girls to my right and the girls to my left are all doing the same thing: sewing on collars. When I finish a shirt, I throw it to the girl behind me. She sews buttonholes. Then she throws it to the row behind her. The girls on that row do finishing stitches. There's rows and rows of us on the eighth floor doing the same thing all day. The air is filled with flying shirts, because there's no time to walk the shirts back and forth.

When the machines are going, my ears are filled up with a kind of clatter that makes me feel like I could go deaf. The machines go like mad all day, and the girls stay hunched over their shirt-waists and don't say much. The boss don't like it if we talk.

Little Mary is a cleaner. Her job is to trim off the threads left on the shirtwaists by the operators. She's over in the children's corner with dozens of other girls. None of 'em is older than eight, and most of 'em are just five or six, like my Mary. All day long, the boss brings over piles and piles of shirts for the cleaners to trim. After the little girls trim the shirts, they put 'em in big boxes so that the examiners can look 'em over.

If the factory inspector comes, the children hide in the big boxes under all the shirts. The boss always knows when the inspectors are coming, so he can wait 'til the last minute before throwing the little ones into the boxes. They have to stay quiet under all the shirts for minutes or hours, depending. Mary says it's hot and dark in the box and that the littler ones cry without making a sound.

We work from 7:00 in the morning to 8:00 at night every day, with a half-hour lunch break at noon. We don't get paid for the break, so I keep working at my machine. Emily takes Mary, and they sit in the corner and have their bread. The peddler comes in at noon with hot rolls, but we have no money for rolls. My girls eat their dark bread without complaining. They're good girls. Patrick and I are trying to make a better life for them.

I worry about Emily and Mary at the factory. There's no windows in our section and no sunlight. There's dust everywhere. Sometimes you can barely get a breath of air because the dust is so thick. On the seventh floor, the windows have to be kept open to let out the steam from the pressers. So they get flies. We have rats on the eighth floor, so it all evens out. (Mary got bit by a rat last week.)

My mother taught me to read and write before I left Ireland. I want do the same for my girls, but there ain't time. Emily tries to help Mary a bit with her letters, but Emily's penmanship ain't so good, so it's a trial for her. Patrick and I, we dream that the girls might go to school.

When I'm at my machine, I'm so hungry for sleep that I could faint. There's a song that the girls used to sing at their machines that begins with "I would rather sleep than eat," but the boss didn't like it, so now we keep quiet. Mostly all we hear is the clatter of the machines, and sometimes we hear one of the children crying in the children's corner. If they cry, they get fired, so mostly the children are quiet too.

*　　*　　*

On March 25, 1911, a fire started on the eighth floor of the Triangle Shirtwaist Company. The fire quickly spread upward to the two top floors of the building. Because factory doors were locked from the outside during the day, the workers had no way to escape. Many jumped from the windows to their deaths. That day 146 people died, many of them children.

People were horrified by the fire and what they learned about working conditions inside the Triangle Shirtwaist Company. Their outrage led to a series of improvements in working conditions in New York and elsewhere. Politicians, reformers, and the workers themselves insisted on new health and safety legislation and child labor laws.

QUESTIONS TO CONSIDER

1. What is your opinion of the working conditions in the Triangle Shirtwaist Company?

2. Why do you suppose sweatshop workers rarely complained about the work or quit to find better jobs?

3. If you had been a reformer in the 1900s, what recommendations would you have made to improve the lives of sweatshop workers?

Mother Jones: One Woman's Fight for Labor
by Betsey Harvey Kraft

Irish-born Mary Harris "Mother" Jones was one of the most extraordinary figures of the American labor movement. Betsey Harvey Kraft's biography presents the career of this tireless union organizer.

We Shall Not Be Moved: The Women's Factory Strike of 1909
by Joan Dash

In 1909, 30,000 female garment workers struggled to end terrible working conditions and to form a trade union of their own. Joan Dash presents an account of the first strike of women in American history.

Big Annie of Calumet: A True Story of the Industrial Revolution
by Jerry Stanley

Annie Clemenc was the 6-foot 2-inch wife of a Croatian copper miner in Calumet, Michigan. When the miners went on strike in 1913, "Big Annie" and the other wives became part of the strike. Jerry Stanley tells the story of their brutal fight for better working conditions.

Industrialization
and the End
of the Frontier

"Half a World Behind Each Back"

BY WALTER HAZEN

What was it the Engines said,
Pilots touching—head to head
Facing on a single track,
Half a world behind each back?

Many years have passed since **Bret Harte** wrote those words. He was talking about the completion of the first **transcontinental** railroad, which crossed this great nation of ours.

People and Terms to Know

Bret Harte—(1836–1902) U.S. author who wrote many stories about life in the West.

transcontinental—crossing a continent. The transcontinental railroad provided a continuous passage from California to the East Coast.

Directors of the Union Pacific are shown in 1866 beside a marker indicating the 100th meridian, eastern border of the Great Plains.

The date was May 10, 1869. The place was **Promontory**, Utah. Yes, I was there. I helped build that railroad. What a fine day it was! Workers of the Central Pacific and Union Pacific railroads cheered as a golden spike was hammered in, connecting the tracks. Now the nation was joined from west to east. I was so proud that my heart almost burst from my chest!

We were both eighteen and eager for all the adventure we could find.

My part of the story starts in the summer of 1864. Sean and I had landed in New York City a few months before. Ah, yes, we were full of hope and eager to make our fortune. But there were no jobs for the Irish. Many people in America didn't like Catholics like us at that time. I spent weeks knocking on doors and getting the brush-off. Our money was gone, and our bellies were stuck to our backbones. So Sean and I headed westward. Soon we were working as railroad laborers for the Union Pacific. We were both eighteen and eager for all the adventure we could find. (As things turned out, we found adventure aplenty!)

People and Terms to Know

Promontory—place where the builders of the Central Pacific and Union Pacific railroads met on May 10, 1869, completing the first transcontinental railroad. Promontory is near the Great Salt Lake in Utah. A promontory is a high point of land stretching out into the water.

The Union Pacific got off to a slow start. The Central Pacific started laying tracks eastward from Sacramento, California, in January 1863. We did not begin at Omaha, Nebraska, until 1865. We knew that somewhere along the way the tracks being laid by the two companies would meet.

Most of the workers for the Union Pacific came from Europe, mostly Ireland. Some among us were veterans of the Civil War. We heard that almost all of the workers on the Central Pacific side were Chinese. Some were from California, having come from China years before. Others were brought in straight from China to work on the railroad.

We heard lots of stories about the Chinese. They worked hard, we heard, but some thought they were a little "peculiar." People on our crews didn't care a whole lot about being clean and eating fancy foods. We went about in our dirty clothes and ate our beef and beans. But we heard these Chinese took a bath every day. Yeah! They made bathtubs of empty whiskey kegs and jumped right in. And they ate things like dried fish, dried fruits, and dried seaweed! Can you believe it?

It didn't take long for Sean and me to have enough adventures for a lifetime. We worked through awful heat in the summer and awful cold in the winter. Stampeding buffalo gave us a few close calls. But Indians scared us the most. We were not long out of Nebraska before the **Sioux** and **Cheyenne** started attacking us all the time. At a place called Plum Creek, the Cheyenne pried up some rails and made a freight train jump the track. We had to watch for attacks every day.

Young as I was and not knowing the ways of America, I asked my foreman one day about the Indians. Why were they trying to stop the railroad?

"Ha!" he answered. "Those Indians are no fools. They can see what's going to happen. This railroad will bring more settlers. And the settlers will drive them out. You can't blame them for trying to stop us."

We had our problems, for sure, as we slowly worked our way west. But the Chinese had it worse. A Chinese worker told me about it.

People and Terms to Know

Sioux—group of American Indian tribes living on the plains of the northern United States.

Cheyenne—tribe of American Indians of the Great Plains, now living in Montana and Oklahoma.

▲

This photograph shows the Central Pacific construction camp on April 1, 1869, shortly before the completion of the first transcontinental railroad.

"Hundreds of my people died working for the Central Pacific," Lin Shao told me. "Some died from hard work. Others were buried under <u>avalanches</u>. But I think more people got hurt and killed digging the tunnels. That was the worst part."

Lin Shao told me stories about blasting through the <u>Sierra Nevada</u>. They'd lower him over the side of a cliff in a basket to drill holes in the rock. Then they'd put explosives in the holes to blast away part of the mountain.

People and Terms to Know

avalanches—rapidly falling masses of ice and rock that slide down mountains.
Sierra Nevada—mountain range in eastern California.

"**Nitroglycerin**, they called it," Lin Shao continued. "It was very powerful. There were many accidents. Yet we blasted about nine tunnels through the Sierras. We also had to build bridges over canyons. It seemed impossible to do some of these things."

But they overcame these problems. On the last day of work, in April 1869, the Chinese laid a record ten miles of track. Lin Shao said it all resulted from a bet between the work boss of the Central Pacific and an official of the Union Pacific. The bet was over which crew could lay the most track in a single day. The Chinese won, and their boss collected $10,000.

I felt sorry for Lin Shao and the other Chinese at the celebration at Promontory on May 10. A lot of important people were there from both railroads. When the two train engines—the Central Pacific's Jupiter and the Union Pacific's No. 19—touched **cowcatchers**, everybody cheered. They broke bottles of champagne over both engines. They gave speeches and congratulated the workers—all the workers except the Chinese, that is. Nobody praised them at all.

People and Terms to Know

Nitroglycerin—explosive liquid used in making dynamite and medicines.
cowcatchers—metal frames once used on the front of locomotives to clear the tracks of obstacles.

We were finished then and out of jobs. As time went by, we could see how important our work was. The transcontinental railroad connected the two coasts. Now people could travel much more easily and move themselves and their things to the West. Business and industry could grow too. With the railroad, manufacturers could sell their goods all over the country.

A few months after the railroad was completed, I read that the nation learned about what took place at Promontory from a telegraph message. It read:

"THE LAST RAIL IS LAID. . . . THE LAST SPIKE IS DRIVEN. . . . THE PACIFIC RAILROAD IS COMPLETED!"

QUESTIONS TO CONSIDER

1. What did Bret Harte mean when he wrote, "Half a world behind each back"?

2. What problems faced the workers of the Union Pacific and Central Pacific railroads?

3. How did the needs of the settlers conflict with the needs of the Plains tribes during this period? What happened?

4. Why do you think that the contributions of Chinese workers were not recognized at the Promontory celebration?

5. In what ways was the transcontinental railroad important to America?

Ten Mile Day: And the Building of the Transcontinental Railroad
by Mary Ann Fraser

On April 28, 1869, Chinese workers laid a record-breaking ten miles of track to win a $10,000 bet for their boss. Mary Ann Fraser uses this famous episode as a focus for her history of the building of the transcontinental railroad.

The Great Railroad Race: The Diary of Libby West
by Kristiana Gregory

Kristiana Gregory's historical novel describes the building of the transcontinental railroad as seen through the eyes of 14-year-old Libby West, daughter of a reporter who follows the railroad.

Full Steam Ahead: The Race to Build a Transcontinental Railroad
by Rhoda Blumberg

Rhoda Blumberg presents a detailed account of one of the most gigantic construction projects in history.

Cornelius Vanderbilt, Robber Baron

BY DIANE WILDE

"Fascinating fellow!" exclaimed Edmond Harrison. He was sitting in his study in his New York City apartment, drinking coffee and reading the morning edition of the *New York Daily Tribune*. It was March 23, 1878.

His young son-in-law, Richard, sitting across from him, looked up from his section of the paper. Richard asked, "Who are you talking about?"

"**Cornelius Vanderbilt**," Harrison replied. "He died last year but they're still quoting him in the paper. For example, he said, 'I've been insane on the

---

People and Terms to Know

Cornelius Vanderbilt—(1794–1877) U.S. businessman who made a fortune in shipping and railroads. Vanderbilt later gave $1 million of his fortune to Vanderbilt University in Nashville, Tennessee.

Photograph of Cornelius Vanderbilt.

subject of moneymaking all my life.' That certainly was true. He didn't care about much else."

"I heard that he grew up on Staten Island, as you did," said Richard.

"It's true. I knew him in school," said Harrison. "Of course, I've watched his career with great interest all my life. We called him 'Corneel' when he was a boy."

"Really!" Richard leaned forward. "I didn't realize that you knew Vanderbilt personally! Is it true that he didn't finish elementary school? How in the world did he get such wealth and power?"

"Well, Richard, it's quite a story," said Harrison. "My old school friend turned out to be one of the most famous **robber barons** of all time." Harrison settled back in his chair, lit his pipe, and began the tale.

*　　*　　*

People and Terms to Know

robber barons—American men of the late 1800s who became powerful in industry or finance, often by illegal means.

"Everyone said Corneel took after his mother, Phebe. He made decisions easily and was careful with money, as she was. Like her, he didn't like moral weakness in others. As today's paper quotes him, 'The secret of my success is that I mind my own business. And I never tell anybody what I'm going to do until I've done it.'

"Vanderbilt was two years younger than I. He grew up on the family farm in Stapleton, on Staten Island, just across the bay from New York City. In those days, Staten Island was a farming community, the garden market for the city's port and trade center.

"Vanderbilt's father, also named Cornelius, had two businesses. He ran the family farm, and he also had a ferry business, carrying farm produce across the bay to the heart of New York City, on Manhattan Island. It was that time after the Revolutionary War when there was a **depression**. Many people were in need. The Vanderbilt family was poor, but farm life was clean and healthy compared to the poverty of the city.

People and Terms to Know

depression—severe slowdown in business activity. During a depression, people cannot find jobs, don't have enough money to buy goods, and there is widespread poverty.

"As I said, I knew Vanderbilt in school. He didn't like it. When he was eleven, he quit school to work full time for his father. He didn't care for farming either. But he liked to work on the water. I heard that it bothered him that his father did not focus on one job—either farming or selling produce.

"Vanderbilt was a tall and energetic young man. He was restless. Just before he turned seventeen, he borrowed $100 from his mother and started his own business. He bought his own boat and began to carry goods to New York City. The first summer, he worked from early morning until late at night. He paid back the $100 and gave $1,000 more to his family.

"At nineteen, Vanderbilt married and started a family. He spent the next twenty years building up his shipping business. He carried goods around the New York area and beyond—north to Massachusetts and south to the Carolinas. A government contract that he obtained during the **War of 1812** helped him expand. He got the nickname 'The Commodore' at this time because he had the largest ship on the Hudson River.

People and Terms to Know

War of 1812—(1812–1814) unpopular conflict with Great Britain. It was a response to shipping restrictions brought about by the British war with France and to the Canadian British arming of the Shawnee chief Tecumseh.

"Vanderbilt became the greatest shipping power of his day. He built more than thirty ships and operated at least 100. During the California gold rush of 1849, he got wealthy because he had shortened the route between New York City and San Francisco. His ships went by way of Central America instead of around the tip of South America.

"Vanderbilt was rich, but he didn't make it into New York society. The Vanderbilts lived in Manhattan for a while, but society people considered Cornelius Vanderbilt very vulgar. So he built a mansion on Staten Island, where he felt most at home.

"In 1862, Vanderbilt became interested in a new up-and-coming industry, railroads. He was an expert on shipping by now. Shipping passengers and goods by water was very similar to shipping them on railroad trains over land. There was a natural connection between the two industries.

"Vanderbilt became a director on the board of the Long Island Railroad. He set up his own steamboats to carry Long Island freight and passengers to and from Connecticut. Then he began to buy railroads. His power grew, both in shipping and in railroads. It was the Civil War, however, that really made his fortune. During a war, demands for both supplies and transportation are very urgent. In less than twenty years, Vanderbilt increased his fortune more than 100 times.

"Over the years, Vanderbilt did many things that were against the law. He was asked about it once and said, 'What do I care for the law? I got the power, ain't I?' He knew the power of money—and he used it. For this reason, Vanderbilt is considered the first of the robber barons.

"It was the Civil War, however, that really made his fortune."

"Powerful, hard-driving men like **Andrew Carnegie** and **John D. Rockefeller** were called robber barons too. There were others. To these men, making money was more important than the law. Some of them got mixed up in illegal dealings with Boss Tweed, the head of New York City's corrupt government.

People and Terms to Know

Andrew Carnegie—(1835–1919) Scottish-born U.S. industrialist who made a fortune in the steel industry. Carnegie gave much of his wealth to charities and set up public libraries throughout the United States.

John D. Rockefeller—(1839–1937) U.S. industrialist who entered the oil industry as a young man and built Standard Oil by combining other companies. Later on, Rockefeller set up several charitable foundations.

▲

This cartoon shows Cornelius Vanderbilt's son William, along with Cyrus W. Field (bottom left) and Jay Gould (bottom right), as together forming a giant that controls American railroads.

"Vanderbilt's wife died in 1868. A year later, he married a thirty-year-old woman. He was seventy-five. He was eighty-two when he died, and he left over $100 million. Most of it went to one of his sons, William Henry Vanderbilt. William Henry was a lot like his father. Once a reporter asked him if railroads should be run for the good of the public. William Henry answered, 'The public be damned!'"

*   *   *

"Well, Richard, what do you think?" said Harrison. "Is this Vanderbilt a man to be admired—or not?"

"Not an easy question!" Richard replied. He paused and turned to gaze out the window. "Great ability is admirable. And so is a fortune of more than $100 million! But should we admire the man? I'll have to think about it."

QUESTIONS TO CONSIDER

1. What personal qualities do you think helped Cornelius Vanderbilt succeed?

2. What reasons does the story give for why a person could make a fortune in industries like shipping, railroads, steel, and oil during the late 1800s?

3. What historical events helped Vanderbilt to build his businesses? How did they help?

4. What qualities do you admire and not admire in Cornelius Vanderbilt? What do you think of his views on wealth and power?

The Gunfight at the O.K. Corral

BY FITZGERALD HIGGINS

Wyatt Earp loved ice cream. I guess that's not the sort of thing most people would expect a tough lawman to like, but he did. When he lived in **Tombstone**, Arizona, his favorite ice cream parlor was on Fourth Street, just a short distance from the O.K. Corral. I used to see him there a lot. It was my favorite place too. I had stopped by for some ice cream on the afternoon of October 26, 1881, when the Earp brothers and **Doc Holliday** shot it out with

---

People and Terms to Know

Wyatt Earp (urp)—(1848–1929) famous lawman in Dodge City, Kansas, and Tombstone, Arizona.

Tombstone—Arizona mining town that grew rapidly after silver was discovered there in 1877.

Doc Holliday—John Holliday (1850–1887), dentist, gambler, and gunman; friend of the Earps.

The night before Virgil Earp and Tom McLaury shot it out at the O.K. Corral, they spent hours playing poker at Tombstone's Occidental Saloon with Ike Clanton and County Sheriff John Behan.

the Clantons and McLaurys behind the O.K. Corral. That's how come I saw the whole thing.

I guess ice cream is not the sort of thing most people would expect to find in a tough mining town like Tombstone either. But in its heyday in the 1880s, Tombstone had a lot of big-city frills—fancy hotels, shops, and restaurants, theaters, a photo studio, tennis courts, and a bowling alley. Of course, it also had the Wild West stuff. There were a lot of saloons and drinking and gambling and guns. So there were lots of brawls too.

A rough crowd known as the Cowboys caused much of the trouble. They were suspected of cattle rustling and stagecoach robberies. What was certain was that, with their drunken fights, they made Tombstone a dangerous place to live. A sad example occurred one night just about a year before the gunfight at the O.K. Corral. Some drunken Cowboys were shooting up the town, and Fred White, Tombstone's **marshal**, tried to stop them. He got shot and died the next day. Fred was a nice guy. It was a real shame.

People and Terms to Know

marshal—U.S. federal law officer.

The Clantons and the McLaurys were Cowboys. They were two sets of brothers—Ike and Billy Clanton, and Tom and Frank McLaury. They were ranchers, but probably a lot of the cattle on both their places originally had other men's **brands**.

Despite Wyatt's taste for ice cream, the Earp brothers were not choirboys.

Virgil Earp, Wyatt's big brother, had been Fred White's deputy. Now he took over the marshal's job. Wyatt became his deputy. Despite Wyatt's taste for ice cream, the Earp brothers were not choirboys. In addition to serving as lawmen, they had supported themselves as saloonkeepers and gamblers and **bounty hunters**.

No choirboy could have policed Tombstone. Virgil was one tough lawman, which is what the town needed. Under him, things quieted down real quick. It looked as if Tombstone was going to get more or less civilized. But if you listened to town gossip, there was talk that the Cowboys were just

---

People and Terms to Know

brands—identifying marks burned into the hides of cattle.

bounty hunters—those who pursue a criminal or fugitive to get the reward that is offered. As they could often get the reward whether the person was "dead or alive," sometimes they were little more than hired killers.

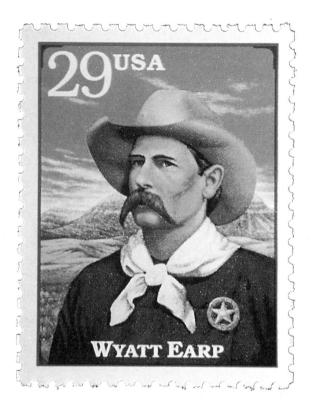

▲

Wyatt Earp has been honored with a postage stamp.

biding their time. They were gonna clean out the
Earps when they got a chance.

Early in September 1881, the Bisbee stagecoach
was robbed. Virgil, Wyatt, and their kid brother
Morgan went after the thieves. The two men the
Earps arrested were both friends of the Cowboys,
and that just made 'em madder at the brothers.

On the night before the gunfight, Ike Clanton ran into Doc Holliday, and the two of them traded insults. It didn't amount to much. Everybody knew that Ike was a loudmouth. And nothing more happened that night.

Next morning, though, Ike kept up his threats, and somewhere he had got a rifle. He went around waving it and saying that as soon as the Earps and Doc Holliday showed themselves on the street, there would be a fight. Wyatt and Morgan woke Virgil up, telling him about Ike. Virgil got dressed, and the brothers went out to look for Ike. Wyatt went one way, and Virgil and Morgan went another.

Shortly before one o'clock, Virgil Earp and his brother found Ike on Fourth Street, still with the rifle in his hand. Virgil walked over to him, grabbed the rifle, and hit Ike over the head with the long barrel of his revolver. Ike went down, and the marshal hauled him off to the police court, where Ike was fined $25 for carrying a weapon. Meanwhile, Wyatt had run into Tom McLaury and slapped him around a bit. By now it was about two o'clock.

Around 2:30, the Clantons and McLaurys and a friend of theirs, Billy Claiborne, had gathered over at the O.K. Corral. Shortly afterward, I saw the Earp brothers and Doc Holliday come walking down Fourth Street. As they strode by, the wind blew open Doc's coat, and I could see that he had a shotgun. Virgil Earp, for some odd reason, was carrying a walking stick. The four men turned the corner into Fremont Street and walked toward the rear entrance of the O.K. Corral. I left my ice cream on the counter and followed after them to see what would happen.

> *The wind blew open Doc's coat, and I could see that he had a shotgun.*

At about 2:45, the Earps and Holliday walked into the small lot at the rear entrance of the O.K. Corral, where the Cowboys were gathered. The nine men faced each other. The two groups made a striking contrast. The Cowboys were dressed in their usual gaudy style—in fancy shirts and silk neckerchiefs, their pants tucked into their boots. The Earps and Holliday were formally dressed—as they usually were—in white shirts and ties, long black coats, and black trousers that covered their boots.

At this point, the county **sheriff**, John Behan, made an attempt to head off the fight that everyone in town knew was coming. First he talked to the Cowboys, and then he came over and said something to the Earps. But it was too late for talk.

There's a lot of confusion about what happened next, but everyone who was there agrees that Virgil Earp said, "Throw up your hands, boys. I have come to disarm you." Suddenly two shots were fired so close together that they sounded like one. There was quiet for a second or two, and then all hell broke loose.

"Throw up your hands, boys. I have come to disarm you."

For the next thirty seconds it sounded like a particularly noisy Fourth of July. Doc Holliday fired his shotgun at Tom McLaury. Tom was hit in the side and fell, but raised himself and fired again before he died. Frank McLaury was hit but kept on shooting, wounding Doc Holliday in the hip. Doc and Morgan Earp shot back, both hitting Frank, who staggered out into the middle of Fremont Street and fell dead. Virgil Earp switched his cane to his left hand, pulled his gun,

People and Terms to Know

sheriff—county law officer.

and blazed away until he was hit in the leg and fell. Billy Clanton was wounded, but kept on shooting. Morgan was hit in the shoulder. Ike Clanton, who had started the whole thing, ran away. So did Billy Claiborne. And where was Wyatt? He just stood amid all the gunsmoke as cool as a cucumber, firing off shot after shot as if he were taking target practice. He wasn't even scratched.

When it was all over, Tom and Frank McLaury and Billy Clanton lay dead. Virgil and Morgan Earp and Doc Holliday were wounded. Sheriff Behan came out of the photography studio next door where he had been taking cover during the shootout. He went up to Wyatt and said, "I'll have to arrest you." Wyatt told him, "I won't be arrested today. I am right here and am not going away." Then Wyatt added, "You lied to me. You told me those men were disarmed."

As you might expect, there was quite an uproar over the killings. The headline in the *Tombstone Epitaph* the next day screamed, "Three Men Hurled into Eternity." The gunfight was even reported in *The New York Times*. After one of our local undertakers had tidied them up, the bodies of Billy Clanton and the McLaury brothers were propped up in his window beneath a sign that said, "Murdered in the Streets of Tombstone." Townsfolk who had felt we were becoming a civilized community were none too happy about the publicity. Our fair city had lived up to its name.

*   *   *

Opinion in Tombstone over whether the Earps and Holliday were justified in the killings was sharply divided. There was an **inquest**, but the judge dismissed murder charges against them.

Tombstone itself didn't last too long after the gunfight at the O.K. Corral. Water began to seep into the silver mines that had made the town wealthy. In 1886 there was a bad fire. In a few more years, "the town too tough to die" was pretty much dead. It survives largely as a sad example of how hard it was to build community life in the early West. To combat lawless groups such as the Cowboys, frontier towns had to turn to men like the Earps and Doc Holliday, who were themselves violent.

People and Terms to Know

inquest—judicial inquiry into a matter, usually held before a jury, especially into the cause of a death.

Who Shot First?

At the inquest held after the gunfight at the O.K. Corral, two witnesses gave different accounts of who had fired first.

Inquest Testimony by R. F. Coleman

"On reaching Fremont street I saw Virgil Earp, Wyatt Earp, Morgan Earp and Doc Holliday, in the center of the street, all armed. . . . I heard Virgil Earp say, 'Give up your arm; or throw up your arms.' There was some reply made by Frank McLaury, but at the same moment there were two shots fired simultaneously by Doc Holliday and Frank McLaury, when the firing became general, over thirty shots being fired."

Inquest Testimony by Wesley Fuller

"The Earps and Holliday were on the corner of Fourth and Allen streets when I saw them armed. Virgil Earp had a shotgun, double barreled; the others had six-shooters. . . . I heard some one say, 'Throw up your hands!' Billy Clanton threw up his hands and said, 'Don't shoot me; I don't want to fight!' At the same time, the shooting commenced. I did not see Ike Clanton at that time; I did not see Frank McLaury. The Earp party fired the first shot; two shots were fired right away; they were almost together, I think they were both pistol shots. Both parties then commenced firing rapidly."

QUESTIONS TO CONSIDER

1. How would you describe life in Tombstone in the early 1880s?

2. What kind of men were the Cowboys?

3. What did the narrator mean when she said that "the Earp brothers were not choir boys"? What kind of men were the Earps?

4. What led to the gunfight at the O.K. Corral?

5. Why do you think it was so difficult to maintain law and order in frontier towns such as Tombstone?

Yellin' Mary Ellen: The Voice of the Populists

BY JUDITH LLOYD YERO

T̲hey called her "The Red Dragon of Kansas," "The Wichita Cyclone," or "Yellin' Mary Ellen." These names all described a Kansas woman of the late 1800s. **Mary Elizabeth Lease**, the daughter of Irish immigrants, was a powerful speaker for the rights of working people.

Mary Elizabeth Clyens was born in 1850. Her father and brother fought for the Union army in the Civil War. Both were killed. All her life, Mary

---

People and Terms to Know

Mary Elizabeth Lease—(1850–1933) popular Kansas public speaker of the late 1800s. Lease helped a number of Populist candidates, including a governor of Kansas, to win elections.

Elizabeth blamed the Democrats for the war that had destroyed her family and left her poor.

At the age of fifteen, Mary Elizabeth graduated from school and began teaching in Pennsylvania. Even at that early age, she spoke out for what she believed. She tried to convince her fellow teachers to demand higher pay. When that failed, she moved to Kansas, where teachers were paid more.

In 1873, Mary Elizabeth married Charles Lease. Unlike other women of her time, she chose to use the name Mary Elizabeth Lease rather than Mrs. Charles Lease. Over the next ten years, she gave birth to four children. Eventually, her husband failed at farming. But she found time to study law at home. "I used to improve every moment. I have often kneaded bread or washed dishes with some newspaper article of interest pinned to the wall in front of me that I should waste no time in digesting its contents."

Lease's hard work was rewarded. In the 1880s, she was admitted to the Kansas bar as a lawyer. Her reasons for studying law were ambitious. "I had studied the law like an honest Abe Lincoln," she once said. Lease's dream was "to fit myself to head the greatest corporation of all as president of the

United States. In that position, I could have been the advocate of the poor man politically and economically."

Lease soon decided that she didn't have the kind of mind necessary to "out-trick the brainy corporation lawyers." But she did find her real gift. When she spoke, people listened! For the rest of her life, Lease used that gift to support many causes. One of her favorites was the plight of farmers.

Lease soon decided that she didn't have the kind of mind necessary to "out-trick the brainy corporation lawyers."

After the Civil War, many American farmers started to use farm machinery. They could farm more efficiently this way, but the costs were high. They had to buy the machines and keep them in repair. Land prices started going up too. Farmers had to take out loans to cover the costs of land and machinery. They dreamed of paying off their loans and making a profit. But bank interest rates were high. So were the railroad charges for shipping their crops. Bad weather or poor crops could bring ruin to farming families.

▲

In this print, a figure representing the Grange, a farmers' organization, tries to waken people to the danger of the railroads' control of the American economy.

Farmers organized to demand protection and help from the government. In the Midwest in 1892, farmers formed their own political party. They became known as **Populists**.

Mary Elizabeth Lease was one of the Populists' strongest supporters. In the election of 1890, she traveled around the country whipping up support for pro-farm candidates.

People and Terms to Know

Populists—political party (officially, People's Party) made up mostly of Midwestern farmers. Populists were concerned over low crop prices, crop failures, unfair loan interest rates, and marketing costs. Several Populist candidates were elected to Congress and many to local offices, but the party never received national support.

For the next six years, Lease helped many local Populist candidates get elected. She was the delight of the new party. One reporter said, "She had a thunderous voice. She could make herself heard for a great distance, and she was one of the finest public speakers I ever heard . . . her talks were shot through with fire and vigor." Another supporter said, "She hurls sentences as [the ancient Roman god] Jove hurled thunderbolts."

"Wall Street owns the country."

One of Lease's most famous speeches blamed the investors and bankers of **Wall Street** for the problems of the working people. "Wall Street owns the country. It is no longer a government of the people, for the people, and by the people, but a government of Wall Street, by Wall Street, and for Wall Street. The great common people of this country are slaves. . . ."

Observers noted that Lease had an almost hypnotic control over her audiences. One reporter said, "She could recite the multiplication table and set a crowd hooting or hurrahing at her will." Lease also was very well informed about issues.

People and Terms to Know

Wall Street—street in New York City on which the major banks and investment houses are located. The term *Wall Street* sometimes is used to symbolize wealthy business interests.

But she was a favorite target for those who wanted women to stay at home. After she helped defeat a Republican candidate in 1890, many critics attacked her. A reporter for a Republican paper called her "hideously ugly in feature and foul of tongue. . . ." Others called her a "**harpy**" and a "petticoated smut-mill." Some changed her middle name and called her "Yellin' Mary Ellen."

Lease's critics noted that, over time, she often supported both sides of issues. They were right. At one time or another, she spoke both for and against Republicans and Democrats. She once gave a speech supporting **socialism** too. She backed **Prohibition** at one point, and then later said that she couldn't understand what all the fuss was about. She also spoke out for a woman's right to vote, and then later denied it. "You know I never went in much for that sort of thing," she said.

People and Terms to Know

harpy—in Greek mythology, a very ugly creature that was part woman and part bird. Harpies were said to steal food and carry off the souls of the dead.

socialism—political system in which workers share in the ownership of farms, factories, and other means of production and also share in the profits.

Prohibition—law against manufacture and sale of alcoholic beverages in the United States.

"Women have enough to be thankful for that they are Americans." Lease even defended her right to change her mind.

What Lease really thought or believed probably will remain a mystery. She was "a woman of one gift," and she used that gift well. Working people loved her, and her opponents hated her. After her death, one former critic admitted that, from 1890 to 1896, Lease was "probably the most powerful person in the state [of Kansas]."

QUESTIONS TO CONSIDER

1. Why do you think that Lease wanted to speak out for farmers and working people?

2. What were Lease's reasons for becoming a lawyer?

3. What did the reporter mean who said, "she could recite the multiplication table and set a crowd hooting or hurrahing at her will"?

4. Why was it important to have a powerful speaker travel around explaining the position of Populist candidates?

5. Why do you think Lease might have changed her positions when arguing about issues?

Children of the Wild West
by Russell Freedman

Growing up on the Western frontier was challenging for pioneer and Native-American children. Award-winning author Russell Freedman tells what their lives were like.

Addie's Dakota Winter
by Laurie Lawlor

Laurie Lawlor's historical novel deals with the hard lives of farm families on the Great Plains in the late 1800s.

Prairie Visions:
The Life and Times of Solomon Butcher
by Pam Conrad

Solomon D. Butcher was a photographer who took thousands of photographs of pioneer families, mostly his neighbors in Custer County, Nebraska. Pam Conrad presents a collection of Butcher's photos and stories about him and frontier Nebraska.

Tragedy at
Wounded Knee

BY JUDITH LLOYD YERO

O n December 28, 1890, U.S. soldiers stopped a band of Sioux Indians who were headed for Pine Ridge Reservation in what is now South Dakota. The soldiers took the Indians and their leader, Chief **Big Foot**, to a cavalry camp at Wounded Knee Creek. An officer said that they could continue their journey the next day.

The next morning, a shot rang out. More shots followed. Before the smoke cleared, more than 200 Indian men, women, and children and about 30 soldiers were dead. Several weeks later, the

---

People and Terms to Know

Big Foot—(c. 1820–1890) Sioux chief known by his people as Spotted Elk. He was considered wise and moderate. He asked the government for a missionary school on the reservation and warned Custer before the Battle of Little Bighorn. (See the note on page 155.)

Plains Indians perform the Ghost Dance on a reservation in about 1888.

commander of the area military praised surviving soldiers for putting down the "hostile savages."

What really happened at Wounded Knee? Since 1890, memories of the Sioux and the soldiers who lived through the event have been collected. This is their story.

*   *   *

In the mid-1800s, thousands of people moved westward, searching for adventure or for land on which they could settle. Most of these settlers came from Europe, where land was scarce and owning land was the key to success. To them, it was natural to claim ownership to a piece of land. But the lands in the western United States were already occupied by Indian tribes that had roamed freely through them for generations.

Land and all things in nature were gifts of the Great Spirit, not things that could be owned.

These Indians saw the land differently. To them, land and all things in nature were gifts of the Great Spirit, not things that could be owned.

Plains Indians made their physical and spiritual home in the lands around the Black Hills of South Dakota. The buffalo herds in this area provided them with food, shelter, and clothing. The Indians used these resources wisely. Unlike the Indians, white men often hunted buffalo carelessly and for sport. The vast herds that supplied the Indians' needs began to disappear. Trails filled with wagons and cavalry cut through the heart of the Indians' homelands. The Sioux, along with the Cheyenne and **Arapaho**, fought against the invaders.

In 1868, the U.S. government asked for peace. The government and several Plains Indian tribes signed the Treaty of Fort Laramie in 1868, agreeing to end their war. In this treaty, the Indians—who always had hunted freely—now agreed to stay within fixed borders. The government promised that only the Indians could use this land and that no one could disturb them. It also promised to give the Indians land for farming and to provide food regularly to any who needed it.

In this treaty, the government promised that no land within the reservation could be taken or sold unless "a majority of all the adult male Indians" who occupied the land agreed. But in the 1870s,

---

People and Terms to Know

Arapaho—tribe of North American Indians living formerly in Colorado and now in Wyoming, Montana, and Oklahoma.

gold was discovered in the Black Hills. Settlers and gold seekers swarmed into many parts of the Indians' reservation. This was illegal, but the government didn't try to stop it.

Instead the government sent Lieutenant Colonel **George Armstrong Custer** and the Seventh Cavalry in January 1876 to protect surveyors and gold prospectors in Sioux territory. Custer tried to wipe out the Sioux in the area. On June 25, 1876, Chief **Sitting Bull** and others defeated Custer and his men in a battle at the **Little Bighorn** River.

By 1890, the old ways of life were all but gone for the Indians. The buffalo that once had provided for their needs had disappeared. Because of a careless government census of the Indians, too little food was sent to the reservations. Government officials also stole some of it. The Sioux were gradually starving to death.

People and Terms to Know

George Armstrong Custer—(1839–1876) U.S. army officer. In the Civil War, Custer was an able leader of Union cavalry. He also distinguished himself in a campaign against the Cheyenne. He was killed at the Battle of Little Bighorn.

Sitting Bull—(c. 1831–1890) chief of the Teton Sioux and head of the Sioux Nation. Sitting Bull led the Sioux in the last major Indian resistance movement in the United States, defeating government troops at Little Bighorn.

Little Bighorn—Montana river that was the site of a battle on June 25, 1876, between Indians and the U.S. Seventh Cavalry. The Sioux and Cheyenne warriors killed Custer and the 210 men with him.

From a distant tribe came word of a movement called the **Ghost Dance**. Its followers believed that the dead ("ghosts") soon would return to drive out the whites and restore the Indians' lands and way of life. To hurry this event, Indians lived by strict rules, performed dances, sang songs, and sought visions. Many Indian tribes, including the Sioux, adopted the ceremony of the Ghost Dance as a way out of their desperate situation.

Many saw the dance as a signal that the Indians were becoming hostile.

Whites didn't understand the spiritual meaning of Indian dances. Therefore, many saw the dance as a signal that the Indians were becoming hostile. Eastern newspapers printed exaggerated stories about the Ghost Dance movement and called the Sioux "savages." A newspaper editor near the Sioux reservation accused these papers of lying and tried to tell the truth. But settlers in the area got nervous. The U.S. government sent thousands of troops to "maintain the peace."

People and Terms to Know

Ghost Dance—religious movement among Indian tribes in the West in the late 1800s; also the name of the dance that is at the center of its rituals. An Indian prophet named Wovoka (c. 1858–1932) believed God had chosen him to spread his message. After the massacre at Wounded Knee, the Ghost Dance movement died out.

Wherever the Ghost Dance was done, Indians were under suspicion.

In early December 1890, Chief Big Foot and his band of about 350 men, women, and children were camped some 150 miles from the Pine Ridge Reservation. Big Foot was known as a wise chief. He truly believed that a lasting peace was possible between the whites and the Sioux. But he knew the presence of government troops broke the Treaty of Fort Laramie.

In mid-December, Big Foot heard shocking news. The U.S. government had sent Indian police to arrest Chief Sitting Bull for encouraging the Ghost Dance movement. Big Foot learned that these police had killed the great chief. Now Big Foot worried for the safety of his band. They had little food, and the government hadn't supplied their fall ration. Their weapons were only good for hunting small game. Now soldiers had been sent to stop their dancing. They had done no wrong, so the band decided to go to the Pine Ridge Reservation. There, **Red Cloud**, chief of the Oglala Sioux, was known to live in peace with the whites.

People and Terms to Know

Red Cloud—(1822–1909) chief of the Oglala Sioux. In 1866 he led attacks on whites who traveled the Bozeman Trail, a shortcut between Wyoming and Montana to western goldfields. However, after this period he was not involved in warfare with the whites.

Wanting to avoid trouble with the soldiers, Big Foot ordered his people to leave in the middle of the night. For three days, the band moved as quickly as they could, trying to reach Pine Ridge before an expected blizzard. On the third night, their hunters were too weak from hunger to search for game, so they slaughtered and ate a few yearling horses. Though Big Foot was seriously ill with pneumonia, he was determined to lead his band to safety.

Big Foot ordered his people to leave in the middle of the night.

On December 28, the starving Sioux trudged across the prairie, hoping to reach Pine Ridge by nightfall. Suddenly, soldiers appeared. Big Foot ordered his people to tie white cloths to the ends of poles—a sign of peace. The mounted soldiers charged at the band. But the Sioux held their white flags high in the air as the old chief had directed.

The soldiers ordered the Indians to come with them to the nearby cavalry camp at Wounded Knee Creek. Not wanting to anger the soldiers, the Indians quickly obeyed their commands. The old chief explained that their visit to Pine Ridge was harmless. They planned to see relatives and attend a council. An army officer promised that they could leave the next day. Chief Big Foot was carried to a tent and treated by army doctors. The rest of the band set up their camp for the night. During the night, the Sioux heard more mounted troops entering the camp and loud celebrations among the soldiers.

The next morning, soldiers ordered the Sioux men to the center of camp and told them to give up their weapons. Lines of soldiers surrounded them. Field cannons, called **Hotchkiss guns**, were moved into place on the hills overlooking the camp. The Seventh Cavalry led by Colonel James Forsyth circled the area.

A few of the Sioux handed over their squirrel guns. Soldiers searched the other men. Some soldiers went to the area where the women were packing. They took axes, knives, and even the awls and needles the women used for beading—anything that might be used as a weapon.

People and Terms to Know

Hotchkiss guns—rapid-fire field artillery that fired shells weighing over two pounds with a range of over 4,000 yards.

Stories differ about what happened next. Those who survived—both Sioux and soldiers—said that Indians didn't fire at the soldiers. Some say that one Ghost Dancer, an outsider to the band, started singing and throwing dirt into the air. A dishonest army translator told the officers that the dancer was threatening the soldiers.

Some say that one Ghost Dancer, an outsider to the band, started singing and throwing dirt into the air.

A soldier tried to take a gun from a young, deaf Indian. The Indian didn't understand and fought to keep his gun. As they struggled, the gun, pointed into the air, discharged. A massacre followed. Cannons fired immediately, killing and wounding most of the men at the center of the camp. Forsyth's cavalry ran down both the wounded and the fleeing women and children. Mothers with small infants pleaded for their lives but were shot. Women and children who hid in a ravine were cut down by one of the cannons. The soldier who manned that gun, with nineteen others, later received the Medal of Honor, the nation's highest award for bravery.

▲

The body of Sioux chief Big Foot lies in the snow at Wounded Knee.

Later studies by Congress suggested that Forsyth and the Seventh Cavalry planned to kill the Indians in revenge for their defeat at Little Bighorn. But, despite pressure from survivors and their families, the U.S. government never took the blame for the killings.

Wounded Knee remains an ugly page in American history.

QUESTIONS TO CONSIDER

1. How would you describe the events at Wounded Knee?

2. What examples of communication problems between Indians and the settlers and soldiers does this story give?

3. Why do you think the government didn't keep the Treaty of Fort Laramie in the 1870s?

4. If you had been a soldier at Wounded Knee, how would you have felt about the Sioux Indians?

5. If you had been a Sioux at Wounded Knee, how would you have reacted to being told to give up your weapons?

Wounded Knee

In his autobiography, a Sioux named Charles Eastman described what he saw when he approached Wounded Knee after the massacre:

Fully three miles from the scene of the massacre we found the body of a woman completely covered with a blanket of snow, and from this point on we found them scattered along as they had been relentlessly hunted down and slaughtered while fleeing for their lives. Some of our people discovered relatives or friends among the dead, and there was much wailing and mourning. When we reached the spot where the Indian camp had stood, among the fragments of burned tents and other belongings we saw the frozen bodies lying close together or piled one upon another.

My Heroes, My People: African Americans and Native Americans in the West
by Morgan Monceaux and Ruth Katcher

The authors present an introduction to the lives of 36 African Americans, Native Americans, and people of mixed race who played a role in the history of the American West.

My Heart Is in the Ground: The Diary of Nannie Little Rose, a Sioux Girl
by Ann Rinaldi

Ann Rinaldi's historical novel presents the experiences of a Sioux girl who is sent away from her family to be a student at Pennsylvania's Carlisle Indian School.

Wounded Knee: An Indian History of the American West
by Dee Brown (adapted by Amy Erlich)

When it appeared in 1970, Dee Brown's account of the destruction of the Indian way of life in the 1800s changed the way people viewed the history of the American West.

Reform

Susan B. Anthony Is Arrested

BY WALTER HAZEN

The date was November 1, 1872. The place was a shoemaker's shop on West Street in Rochester, New York. The event that was about to take place had never before occurred in the United States.

The shoemaker's shop served as the **registration** office in Rochester. People who wanted to vote in the presidential election of 1872 went there to register. As a newspaper reporter, I was there to get an idea of how many people actually planned to vote.

Well, let me tell you one thing. I was as shocked as the registration officials were when a large group of ladies walked through the door. They said they

---

People and Terms to Know

registration—putting one's name on a list; in this case, a list of qualified voters.

Susan B. Anthony stands next to Elizabeth Cady Stanton. The two were leaders in the fight for votes for women.

had come to register to vote. They were led by **Susan B. Anthony**. I knew her well from having covered her earlier activities in the women's **suffrage** movement.

With Susan B. Anthony were her three sisters and twelve other women. Miss Anthony stated that because of the Fourteenth and Fifteenth amendments, they were within their right to register. She pointed out that the Fourteenth Amendment had made them citizens, and as citizens, they could not be kept from voting. The Fifteenth Amendment, she believed, only strengthened their case. It stated that no one could be denied the right to vote because of race or color.

The embarrassed young men at the registration office did not know what to do.

"What do *you* say?" one of them asked another.

"I say it's unlawful," came the response.

At that, Miss Anthony broke in. "And I say it is your duty!" she declared.

People and Terms to Know

Susan B. Anthony—(1820–1906) U.S. leader in the struggle to win the right to vote for women. She was also active in other reform movements.

suffrage—right to vote. The movement to get U.S. women the right to vote began with the Seneca Falls Convention (1848) for women's rights, organized by Elizabeth Cady Stanton and Lucretia Mott.

After some time, the registration officials gave in. Miss Anthony, her sisters, and the other ladies were allowed to register. No one present in the shoemaker's shop, myself included, really thought the women would actually vote four days later.

But they did! And the nation was shocked. On November 5, 1872, they went to their polling places and voted. And they were each arrested. In a later interview, Miss Anthony told me what happened at her home on Thanksgiving Day when a U.S. marshal rang her doorbell.

"I have a warrant for your arrest," he said. "You are charged with voting unlawfully."

Miss Anthony said the marshal was extremely polite and a little embarrassed.

"I have a **warrant** for your arrest," he said. "You are charged with voting unlawfully."

Apparently disappointed at the officer's politeness and his reluctance to make too much of a scene, Miss Anthony asked, "Is this your usual method of serving a warrant?"

People and Terms to Know

warrant—written order giving legal authority to do something.

She said she put out her wrists, wanting to be handcuffed. The more attention that was drawn to her case the better, she thought. But the young marshal would have none of that. His goal was to escort Miss Anthony to the commissioner's office with as little fuss as possible. And that is exactly what he did.

All sixteen of the ladies who had voted on November 5 were fined $100. So were the registrars who had allowed them to vote. But Miss Anthony refused to pay. As a result, she was informed that she would be placed on trial on June 17, 1873. The trial was to be held at the courthouse in the town of Canandaigua. It was not held in Rochester because many people there sympathized with Miss Anthony's cause. The **district attorney** felt that a trial held in Rochester would not be fair.

I traveled to Canandaigua to cover the trial. It was nothing more than a joke. From the start, it was

---

People and Terms to Know

district attorney—official who tries criminal cases in a specific district or area.

clear that Miss Anthony's attorney, Henry Selden, would not be allowed to properly defend her. Nor would the presiding judge, Ward Hunt, let the jury decide the case.

On the second day of the trial, Judge Hunt turned to the jury and ordered them to return a **verdict** of guilty. The jury was stunned. Were they not even to be allowed to discuss the case and decide for themselves? Obviously not.

"Take the verdict, Mr. Clerk," the judge ordered the clerk of the court.

Henry Selden objected vigorously. But the judge rapped and rapped with his gavel and ignored him. "Take the verdict, Mr. Clerk," the judge ordered the clerk of the court.

The clerk then turned to the jury and said, "You say you find the defendant guilty of the offense . . . and so say you all."

The jury had said no such thing. In fact, they had said nothing. They were as confused and puzzled as everyone else in the court. They were really confused when Judge Hunt informed them that their duty was over and they were dismissed.

People and Terms to Know

verdict—decision of a judge or jury in a case of law.

Miss Anthony returned to court the following day for sentencing.

"Have you anything to say before I pronounce your **sentence**?" Judge Hunt asked.

I sensed immediately that the judge regretted having asked that question.

"Yes, your honor," Miss Anthony replied. "I have many things to say, for in your ordered verdict you have trampled underfoot every vital principle of our government." Miss Anthony continued talking, even when the judge ordered her to stop and sit down. She pointed out that her constitutional rights had been ignored and that she had been degraded. She went on until Judge Hunt, his face red with rage, screamed once more for her to stop.

Miss Anthony did not stop and sit down until she had had her say. Then Judge Hunt told her to stand and hear her sentence. "The sentence of the court is that you pay a fine of $100 and the costs of the trial."

"May it please Your Honor, I shall never pay a dollar of your unjust penalty!"

And she never did. And Judge Hunt never ordered her to prison. He knew that if she was

People and Terms to Know

sentence—punishment decided on by a judge.

imprisoned, she could then take her case to a higher court. Such an action would have drawn even more attention to her cause.

Two years after Miss Anthony's trial, women were dealt another setback. In 1875, the U.S. Supreme Court ruled that citizenship, as defined in the Fourteenth Amendment, meant "membership in a nation and nothing more." With that decision, Miss Anthony realized that the only way for women to gain the right to vote was through a new constitutional amendment.

*   *   *

In 1920, fourteen years after the death of Susan B. Anthony, women nationwide were given the right to vote with the passage of the Nineteenth Amendment.

QUESTIONS TO CONSIDER

1. On what basis did Susan B. Anthony believe that women had the right to vote?

2. Why did Anthony want to be handcuffed when she was arrested?

3. Why wasn't Anthony's trial held in Rochester?

4. What was the point of view of the judge?

5. Why wasn't Anthony sent to prison?

6. How was the Supreme Court's ruling of 1875 a setback for women?

Susan B. Anthony: Champion of Women's Rights
by Helen Albee Monsell

Helen Albee Monsell presents an account of the childhood of one of the most famous leaders in the fight for women's rights.

Petticoat Politics: How American Women Won the Right to Vote
by Doris Faber

Doris Faber tells the story of the women's suffrage movement that led to the passage of the 19th Amendment.

So Far from Home: The Diary of Mary Driscoll, an Irish Mill Girl
by Barry Denenberg

One of Susan B. Anthony's goals was to improve the lives of the women and girls who worked in American factories. Barry Denenberg's historical novel presents the experiences of one of these workers. In 1847, Mary Driscoll flees hunger in Ireland to work in the mills of Lowell, Massachusetts.

The Man Who Exposed the Slums

BY MARIANNE McCOMB

The summer I turned seventeen, I had the pleasure of accompanying the gifted journalist <u>Jacob Riis</u> as he made his rounds through the dismal slums of New York. You'll notice that I've used the word *pleasure,* although I know the word is terribly misleading. This was not a *pleasant* summer, by any means. In fact, what I saw in those months with Riis filled my eyes with hot tears and my heart with a burning anger that has never left me. Yet it was such an honor to work alongside the great Jacob Riis. I look back on those months of endless walking, talking, and investigating with a kind of pleasure that I've never again experienced in my career.

People and Terms to Know

Jacob Riis (rees)—(1849–1914) Danish-born U.S. newspaper writer and social reformer.

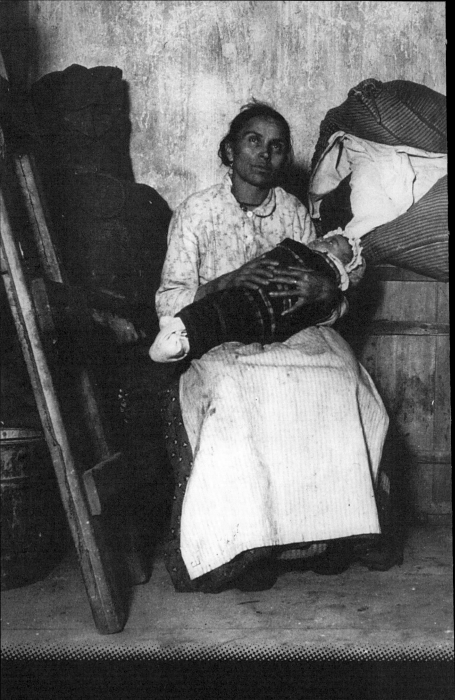

Jacob Riis photographed this Italian mother and her baby in
New York City in 1890.

You may know me by my work. I am a journalist with one of the large New York City papers. Some call me a **muckraker**, but I've been called much worse, so I let it pass. I've been a journalist for almost ten years now. When I was growing up, I planned to be a lawyer. However, my summer with Jacob Riis changed that plan forever.

When I first met him, Riis was researching his explosive book *How the Other Half Lives.* In the spring of 1889, he advertised in the paper for a research assistant to help him. Because I was the only person to answer the ad, he offered me the job at our first meeting. Then he explained the idea for his book and what kind of help he needed.

How the Other Half Lives was to be an **exposé** of life in the slums of New York. Riis had been working on the book for about a year and was almost finished. What he needed at this point, he said, was some information about the children who lived in these slums. He wanted to find out what their lives were like and how they were affected by the poverty that was all around them.

People and Terms to Know

muckraker—American journalist or novelist of the early 1900s who exposed social and political evils.

exposé (EK•spoh•ZAY)—making public of crime, dishonesty, fraud, or something similar.

His plan, he said, was to visit several **tenements** in New York City and talk with the mothers, fathers, and children. This would help him understand why the **infant mortality rate** in the slums was so high. One of every ten babies born in the slums died, he explained. He wanted to find out why.

One of every ten babies born in the slums died, he explained. He wanted to find out why.

We spent the rest of the spring preparing for our interviews. I helped Riis gather his camera equipment, sort through his notes, and decide which tenements to visit. As we worked, he told me the story of his life.

Jacob August Riis was born in Ribe, Denmark, on May 3, 1849. As a child, Riis showed an interest in writing, but he planned a career as a carpenter. At the age of twenty-one, he came to the United States in search of opportunity. Like so many men of his day, he believed he could make a better living in America.

People and Terms to Know

tenements—buildings in a poor section of a city that are divided into sets of rooms in which many different families live.

infant mortality rate—percent of babies who die in a given time period. The rate is usually measured in deaths per thousand infants born in a given year.

Riis discovered on his arrival that an immigrant's life in the United States could be terribly hard. For several long months, he was jobless, hungry, homeless, and very often on the brink of suicide. In 1877, he was fortunate enough to land a job as a police reporter for the New York *Tribune*. His beat was the East Side slum district of New York City.

▲
Jacob Riis photographs a vegetable stand on Mulberry Street in New York's "Little Italy" neighborhood in the 1890s.

Riis spent his nights and days tramping the filthy streets of the East Side. He spoke with the men and women returning home from their long days in the sweatshops. He listened as the police told stories of the terrible crime rate caused by overcrowding. As he poked about these "foul alleys and fouler tenements," he began to get a sense of the horrible poverty and despair that was a part of everyday life on the East Side.

With each sickly child he met and each ramshackle, rat-infested tenement he visited, Riis's anger grew.

With each sickly child he met and each ramshackle, rat-infested tenement he visited, Riis's anger grew. Finally, it was a white-hot rage that threatened to tear him apart. Each time he saw a family of thirteen crammed into a dark, airless, one-room apartment, Riis shook from head to toe with outrage. These people were living like animals, he realized, and they were dying as a result of it.

Riis knew that the poverty he saw on the East Side existed because landlords were greedy, and crooked politicians looked the other way when the unsafe and unsanitary tenements were being built. Each day it seemed, hundreds of immigrants were herded into the East Side slums by rich men who were looking to get richer. By 1889, 22,000 tenements had been built to house a population of 1,093,791.

Finally, after months of walking his beat, Riis could stand it no longer. He began to write stories for the *Tribune* about the plight of these people. He told of the poverty, disease, and filth that slum families coped with every day. In 1888, he began writing a series of articles that eventually would become *How the Other Half Lives*.

What I saw that summer with Riis is almost impossible to describe. I'll never forget the many dark, dreary apartments whose hallways were carpeted in rat droppings. I can still smell the stink of the thin cabbage soups that were cooked over lanterns in rooms with no windows and no ventilation. And I can still see the despair that darkened the faces of the beautiful women and bent the backs of the proud men! I saw all this and so much more.

Like all New York summers, the summer of 1889 was brutally hot. Day after day, great waves of heat rose from the pavement and threatened to knock a grown man flat. In the tenements, the heat climbed up the creaky stairs, one floor at a time, until the whole building was as hot as a cookstove. Thousands of families were forced up to the roofs to try to catch a breath of air. Each morning, there were stories of drowsy men and women who had fallen to their deaths because they had rolled over in their sleep once too often. Hot and tired children lunged for balls or dolls and fell screaming to the pavement below. As the death toll from roof falls mounted, families returned to their airless apartments and prayed for a break in the weather.

The heat climbed up the creaky stairs, one floor at a time, until the whole building was as hot as a cookstove.

Then, in the middle of the summer, the East Side exploded in an **epidemic** of disease. The life of every child in the slum was in danger. It was as if

People and Terms to Know

epidemic—rapid spread of a disease so that many people have it at one time.

Death himself had come to pay a call and had decided at the last minute to spend all his time visiting the innocent children.

Almost overnight, thousands of children were struck down with the measles. In these crowded tenements, one sick child could mean death to ten others. That was how quickly the illness passed from one to another. As their children's fevers rose higher and higher, parents became frantic. There was no medicine to be had and no money to pay for doctors. Gray-faced mothers walked the streets with a feverish infant on each arm. Exhausted fathers comforted delirious little ones as they panted for air and begged for a cold drink.

In other parts of New York, the measles epidemic was easily controlled. Sick children were cared for by attentive doctors who knew the proper treatments. These fortunate babes were usually up and running again after two quiet weeks in bed.

In the East Side tenements, however, the disease was anything but under control. Children began dying by the truckload. Soon white mourning badges fluttered from every other window and door. Child-sized coffins were piled high on the charity boat that made the daily run to the city cemetery.

Jacob Riis, who said he had seen everything, had never seen anything like this. One woman we spoke with lost eight children in the course of four months. The rest of the family—the mother, father, and four remaining children—sat stone-faced as Riis asked his questions. Throughout the interview I was speechless with grief. How could these people live through such a loss? How could they carry on, knowing that the next child and the next and the next might fall dead at their feet at any moment? It was more than I could bear.

By the end of the summer, the measles epidemic had worn itself out. Riis had the material for his book. I had announced to my parents that I no longer planned to study law. Like Jacob Riis, I would use my pen as a weapon in the war against poverty. I would join the other reformers in the city and do what I could to help. I would begin today, I said, and I would not rest until the slums had been cleaned, the tenements had been torn down, and the hungry had been given their fair share of the hearty soups, meats, and stews that bubbled merrily on the other side of town.

QUESTIONS TO CONSIDER

1. What was life like on New York City's East Side during the late 1800s?

2. Why do you think Riis took such a keen interest in the conditions of the immigrants living in the slums?

3. How were journalists and writers such as Riis able to change attitudes about the poor?

4. What could you do if you were to see suffering like the narrator of this story saw?

How the Other Half Lives

In his shocking account of urban poverty, Jacob Riis pictured a slum building on New York's Lower East Side:

Be a little careful please! The hall is dark and you might stumble over the children pitching pennies back there. Not that it would hurt them; kicks and cuffs are their daily diet. They have little else. . . .

Come over here. Step carefully over this baby—it is a baby, [in] spite of its rags and dirt—under these iron bridges called fire-escapes, but loaded down, despite the incessant [constant] watchfulness of the fire-men, with broken household goods, with washtubs and barrels, over which no man could climb from a fire. This gap between dingy brick walls is the yard. That strip of smoke-colored sky up there is the heaven of these people. Do you wonder that the name [of heaven] does not attract them to the churches?

Carry Nation

BY STEPHEN CURRIE

Among the conditions of city life that reformers of the late 1800s and early 1900s tried to change was **alcoholism**. Many poor families suffered, especially when the man in the family spent what little they had on drink. The **temperance movement** tried to solve this problem. One early temperance reformer was **Carry Nation**.

*　　*　　*

People and Terms to Know

alcoholism—disease in which a person feels a physical and psychological craving for alcohol.

temperance movement—organized activity of the 1800s and early 1900s against the sale and drinking of alcoholic drinks.

Carry Nation—(1846–1911) temperance worker who became famous for destroying saloons, first with rocks and bricks and then with hatchets. She was born in Kentucky, but did most of her "smashing" in and around Kansas.

Photograph of Carry Nation with her hatchet and her Bible.

"He is a good man," Mrs. Lewis said helplessly. "At least, he was." Tears slid down her face. I handed her my handkerchief. "But now that he goes to the saloon, I feel that I scarcely know him."

Mrs. Brown shook her head sadly. "Tell us about your husband, my dear."

Mrs. Lewis was a small woman in her late twenties, but she seemed much older. She had a haunted, beaten look that made me want to turn away. This was her first meeting with us.

"We used to be so happy together," she said. "We never had much, but we had each other, and the children—"

"What happened?" I prompted gently.

There was a pause. I looked around our little group: Mrs. Brown, Mrs. Thomas, Mrs. Lewis, and a tall, hatchet-faced stranger in a heavy black cape who sat off to the side. We were of the Temperance Movement. Our goal was to wipe out the **saloons** and to forbid the sale, the manufacture, and the drinking of alcohol. We knew what Mrs. Lewis would say. Thousands of women had the same story.

People and Terms to Know

saloons—places where alcoholic drinks are sold and drunk; taverns or bars.

"First, he stopped coming home on Fridays," Mrs. Lewis began, scarcely above a whisper.

"Paydays," I murmured. "He stopped bringing his pay home?"

"Yes." Mrs. Lewis swallowed. "The children would sit in the window watching for their Pa, but he never came. There was precious little in the house by payday. So we all went to bed hungry. Finally, he would come home drunk and angry, screaming at us. He even would—hit—me sometimes." She hung her head in shame.

> "Paydays,"
> I murmured.
> "He stopped
> bringing his
> pay home?"

We had seen the angry welt on Mrs. Lewis's jaw. I pictured her children, frightened and hungry, listening to this. I felt thankful that my own husband had never taken to drink.

"He has promised to stop the drinking," Mrs. Lewis went on. "But he cannot, or he will not. I do not know which. He was a carpenter, and a good one, but he was so often drunk that he lost his position. No matter, he used to say. He would get another job. And he did. Then he would lose that one. Now he sweeps the floors in the bank, but he has missed three days this week owing to drink,

This 1901 cartoon shows Carry Nation busting up a saloon.

and—and—and I do not know what we shall do."
She cried great gulping sobs.

"There, there, dear. We are so sorry!" Mrs.
Thomas said softly. "Do you know, we are all of us
working to get rid of the saloon."

"But how shall we do it?" I demanded. Anger
pounded in my head, as it so often did when
I heard stories like Mrs. Lewis's. "Shall we write
more letters to the mayor? Shall we sing more
temperance songs?"

In the evenings, we often gathered by the dark
and musty door of the saloon and lifted our voices

in song: "**Father's a Drunkard and Mother Is Dead**"; "The Ruin Rum Hath Wrought"; and "The Saloon Must Go." Singing felt good, but it had never convinced the drunken men inside to go home. "They are not shamed," I said. "They lurch out the door, stinking of alcohol, and they laugh and point at us. Or they never notice us at all."

She was a large woman, perhaps six feet tall. There was something forbidding about her. Her eyes blazed with fury.

At that moment the stranger in the cape stood up. She was a large woman, perhaps six feet tall. There was something forbidding about her. Her eyes blazed with fury. She cleared her throat.

"Alcohol," she said, "kills the living and preserves the dead!"

Mrs. Thomas nodded. "Well spoken, sister—"

"Nation," said the stranger. "Carry Nation is my name." And Mrs. Nation spun a tale in words that stung, words that demanded attention. Her first husband, like Mrs. Lewis's, had been a drunkard.

People and Terms to Know

"Father's a Drunkard and Mother Is Dead"—perhaps the most popular temperance song of the late 1800s. It described the unhappy life of a girl whose family had been destroyed by her father's drinking.

She had left him. She had dedicated her life to the battle against alcohol. She had decided that direct action would be better than song.

She must have been a persuasive speaker, for all four of us soon found ourselves following her down the street toward the saloon.

"I have always wondered what goes on behind this door," whispered Mrs. Thomas nervously. "Now I suppose I shall find out."

Mrs. Nation held tightly to her cape. She strode to the saloon door and rapped sharply.

"Come on in," slurred a voice from the darkness behind. The door creaked open to reveal a little white-haired man.

"Get out of the way," Mrs. Nation cried. "I do not want to strike you, but I am going to break this place up!" And with that she charged forward, wailing like a demon. The man ducked to the side. Mrs. Nation dug beneath her cape. Like an angry giant she pulled out a supply of bricks and rocks and flung these weapons in every direction. Bricks shattered bottles. Stones knocked glasses off their perches. Liquor spilled from the broken containers. It pooled on the wooden counter and the bare floor below.

Mrs. Brown looked shocked.

"Young man," Mrs. Nation cried to the bar-keeper. "Come out from behind that bar. Your mother did not raise you for such a place!" He did not need to be told twice. She climbed up onto the pool table, seized a billiard ball, and heaved it at the mirror behind the bar. There was a crash, and pieces of jagged glass rained down on the floor.

"Good heavens," murmured Mrs. Brown.

Howling with fury, Mrs. Nation smashed a brick into the cash register. Coins scattered all around. She kicked in a barrel that held beer, and the evil liquid foamed out. Men cowered, crying, on the floor. I felt sure that Mrs. Lewis's husband was among them.

"But, Mrs. Nation, this is private property—" Mrs. Thomas began, her eyes as big as saucers.

"Anything that is sinful cannot be lawful," said Mrs. Nation sharply. "If a mother should see a gun pointed at her son, would she break the law to snatch the gun and smash it?"

"Yes," agreed Mrs. Thomas. "But this is not—"

"The saloon is worse than the gun," said Mrs. Nation. "The gun could only destroy the body."

"But you could be arrested," said Mrs. Brown weakly.

"Then I will come out of jail a roaring lion," said Mrs. Nation, "and I will make all hell howl."

I looked at Mrs. Nation. This woman meant what she said, and I thought that perhaps she was right. If liquor is evil, I reasoned, then it must be stopped, and stopped by any means necessary.

"I will come out of jail a roaring lion," said Mrs. Nation, "and I will make all hell howl."

I thought about when we had acted like ladies, calm and polite and well behaved, singing outside the saloon doors. We had been ignored. Had we brought men home to their families? Had we closed down the saloon or given food to starving babies?

In five short minutes, Mrs. Nation had made sure this saloon would not serve liquor for weeks. In five short minutes, she had sent Mrs. Lewis's husband back to his family and saved his job. Joy soared in my heart. I flung the last whole bottle sharply to the floor, where it smashed. Mrs. Nation gave the heavy wooden counter a violent push. But even Carry Nation could not destroy it with her bare hands.

I looked at her face, and I suddenly knew what she should do.

"Next time," I suggested, "you should bring along a hatchet."

QUESTIONS TO CONSIDER

1. Why were the women in the story opposed to alcohol?

2. Why did the women sing songs outside the saloon? What do you think they accomplished by singing?

3. What do you think Carry Nation meant when she said, "The saloon is worse than the gun. The gun could only destroy the body"?

4. What is your opinion of the narrator's statement that evil must be stopped by any means necessary?

5. Why wasn't Carry Nation afraid of going to jail?

Sources

Reconstruction and P. B. S. Pinchback
by Judith Lloyd Yero

The characters in this story are historical figures and the events really happened. Although many of Pinchback's papers were lost after his death and stories of his youth are mainly speculation and legend, a number of his impressive speeches can be found in his biography *Pinckney Benton Stewart Pinchback* by James Haskins (New York: Macmillan Publishing, 1973). The story about his experience with George Devol is from *Forty Years a Gambler on the Mississippi* by George Devol (Austin, TX: Steck-Vaughn, 1967).

Ida B. Wells *by Stephen Currie*

Henry and his father are fictional characters, but Ida B. Wells is a historical figure who really did run the Memphis *Free Speech* and actively sought to end lynching in the United States. To learn more about her, you can read Linda O. McMurry's *To Keep the Waters Troubled: The Life of Ida B. Wells.* (New York: Oxford Univeristy Press, 1998).

In the Land of Jim Crow *by Stephen Feinstein*

The Chicago journalist who narrates this story is a fictional character. So is the publisher, Richard Holdener. But Homer Plessy is a historical figure whose Supreme Court case is one of the nation's most well known. The information about Jim Crow laws and the events told in the story are historically accurate. Sources include *The Strange Career of Jim Crow* by C. Vann Woodward (New York: Oxford University Press, 1974), *America in Black and White: One Nation, Indivisible* (New York: Simon & Schuster, 1997), and *March toward Freedom: A History of Black Americans* by James A. Banks and Cherry A. Banks (Belmont, CA: Fearon Publishers, Inc., 1974).

Gold Mountain *by Diane Wilde*

Foon Lee and the other characters in this story are fictional. The story's description of San Francisco in the late 1800s is historically accurate, as is the information about immigrant Chinese experiences at that time. For more information, see *On Gold Mountain: The One Hundred Year Odyssey of My Chinese-American Family* by Lisa See (New York: Vintage Books, 1996). Other books include *Tales from Gold Mountain: Stories of the Chinese in the New World* by Paul Yee (New York: Groundwood Books, 1999) and *Songs of Gold Mountain: Cantonese Rhymes from San Francisco Chinatown* by Marlon K. Hom (Berkeley, CA: University of California Press, 1992).

Traveling Steerage *by Dee Masters*

The characters in this story are fictional. The events are like those experienced by many immigrants from Russia in the late 1800s. The story is based on the novel *The Promised Land* by Mary Antin (Boston: Houghton Mifflin, 1940) and the short story "How I Found America" in *Hungry Hearts* by Anzia Yezierska (New York: Persea Books, 1985). Both women emigrated to the United States and became successful writers. Two other excellent sources of firsthand accounts are *Coming to America: Immigrants from Eastern Europe* by Shirley Blumenthal (New York: Delacorte, 1981) and *Ellis Island Interviews: In Their Own Words* by Peter Morton Coan (New York: Facts on File, 1997).

A Day at Ellis Island *by Stephen Currie*

The narrator and her family are fictional characters. The description of immigration procedures at Ellis Island is historically accurate. Further information about Ellis Island can be found in *Ellis Island: A Pictorial History* by Barbara Benton (New York: Facts on File, 1985).

Breaker Boys *by Diane Wilde*

Michael, his family members, and friends are fictional characters. The working conditions in Pennsylvania mines at this time are accurately depicted. More information can be found in *The Kingdom of Coal: Work, Enterprise, and Ethnic Communities in the Mine Fields* by Donald L. Miller and Richard E. Sharpless (Philadelphia: University of Pennsylvania Press, 1985).

My Day in the Sweatshop *by Marianne McComb*

The family in this story is fictional, but the Triangle Shirtwaist Co. was a real factory. The working conditions described are historically accurate. Sources include "Letters to Michael and Hugh Owens from P. M. Nowman" in the International Ladies' Garment Workers' Union Archives (Ithaca, NY: Cornell University, Kheel Center for Labor-Management Documentation and Archives), *Good Girl Work: Factories, Sweatshops, and How Women Changed Their Role in the American Workforce* by Catherine Gourley (Brookfield, CT: The Millbrook Press, 1999), and *Out of the Sweatshop: The Struggle for Industrial Democracy* (New York: Quadrangle/New Times Book Company, 1977).

"Half a World Behind Each Back" *by Walter Hazen*

The narrator, his brother, and Lin Shao are fictional characters. The information in the story is historically accurate. Sources for more information about the transcontinental railroad and the age in which it was built include *A History of US: The Age of Extremes* by Joy Hakim (New York: Oxford University Press, 1994). Another source is *The Union Restored* by T. Harry Williams and the editors of *Life*, Volume 6 of the *Life* History of the United States (New York: Time, Incorporated, 1963).

Cornelius Vanderbilt, Robber Baron *by Diane Wilde*

Edmond Harrison and Richard are fictional characters. Cornelius Vanderbilt is a historical figure and the information about his life and quotes attributed to him are historically accurate. Sources include *Commodore Vanderbilt: An Epic of the Steam Age* by Wheaton Lane (New York: Knopf, 1942).

The Gunfight at the O.K. Corral *by Fitzgerald Higgins*

Except for the unnamed narrator, all the people in this story are historical figures. The major source is Allen Barra's *Inventing Wyatt Earp: His Life and Many Legends* (New York: Carroll & Graf, 1998). Another recent book on Wyatt Earp is Casey Tefertiller's *Wyatt Earp: The Life Behind the Legend* (New York: John Wiley & Sons, 1999).

Yellin' Mary Ellen: The Voice of the Populists
by Judith Lloyd Yero

Characters and events in this story are historically accurate. All quotations about Lease are from reporters and newspapers of the time, mainly in Kansas. One of the best sources on Lease is "Mary Elizabeth Lease, Populist Orator: A Profile" (*Kansas History* 1, 1978, pp. 3–15). A biography of Lease can be found in *Queen of Populists: The Story of Mary Elizabeth Lease* by Richard Stiller (New York: HarperCollins Children's Books, 1970).

Tragedy at Wounded Knee *by Judith Lloyd Yero*

This story is based on reports from survivors of the massacre at Wounded Knee, both Sioux and U.S. soldiers. Sources include *The Wounded Knee Massacre: From the Viewpoint of the Sioux* by James H. McGregor, retired U.S. Superintendent of the Pine Ridge Reservation (Rapid City, SD: Fenske Printing Inc., 1940) and *The Winter of 1890: What Happened at Wounded Knee* by Don Huls, which is a collection of articles printed in the Chadron, Nebraska, *Democrat* at the time of the massacre and reprinted in 1974. *Lost Bird of Wounded Knee* by Renee Sansom Flood (New York: Scribner, 1995) includes eyewitness accounts as well as testimony from later investigations. The Laramie Treaty of 1868 is widely available on the Internet.

Susan B. Anthony Is Arrested *by Walter Hazen*

Except for the narrator, all the people in the story are real. The events described are historically accurate. The major source is *Not For Ourselves Alone: The Story of Elizabeth Cady Stanton and Susan B. Anthony* by Geoffrey C. Ward (New York: Alfred A. Knopf, 1999).

The Man Who Exposed the Slums *by Marianne McComb*

The narrator of this story is a fictional character. However, Jacob Riis and the slum conditions depicted in the story are real. The most important source for additional information is *How the Other Half Lives: Studies among the Tenements of New York* by Jacob A. Riis (New York: Dover Publications, Inc., 1971).

Carry Nation *by Stephen Currie*

Carry Nation is a real historical figure and her activities are accurately portrayed. The other women and men in this story are fictional characters. The basic source about Carry Nation is her autobiography, *The Use and Need of the Life of Carry A. Nation, Written by Herself* by Carry Amelia Nation (Topeka, KS: F. M. Steves & Sons, 1908).

Glossary of People and Terms to Know

alcoholism—disease in which a person feels a physical and psychological craving for alcohol.

Anthony, Susan B.—(1820–1906) U.S. leader in the struggle to win the right to vote for women. During her lifetime, she was also active in other reform movements.

Arapaho—tribe of North American Indians living formerly in Colorado and now in Wyoming, Montana, and Oklahoma.

Austria—country in south central Europe that borders Switzerland, Germany, the Czech Republic, Slovakia, Hungary, Slovenia and Italy. Its people speak German.

avalanches—rapidly falling masses of ice and rock that slide down mountains.

Big Foot—(c. 1820–1890) Sioux chief known by his people as Spotted Elk. He was considered wise and moderate. He asked the government for a missionary school on the reservation and warned Custer before the Battle of Little Bighorn.

bounty hunters—those who pursue a criminal or fugitive to get the reward that is offered. As they could often get the reward whether the person was "dead or alive," sometimes they were little more than hired killers.

brands—identifying marks burned into the hides of cattle.

breaker boy—boy who worked in the breaker building near the coal mine, separating coal chunks from pieces of slate and rock.

Carnegie, Andrew—(1835–1919) Scottish-born U.S. industrialist who made a fortune in the steel industry. Carnegie gave much of his wealth to charities and set up public libraries throughout the United States.

carpetbagger—insulting term for Northern politicians, businessmen, and adventurers who came to the South after the Civil War. Some wanted to help blacks, but others sought financial and political opportunities. The name comes from the cheap suitcases made of carpet in which they carried their belongings.

Cheyenne—tribe of American Indians of the Great Plains, now living in Montana and Oklahoma.

Chinatown—neighborhood or section of a city that is inhabited mostly by Chinese people.

Chinese Exclusion Act—(1882) federal law that banned all Chinese except students, teachers, merchants, tourists, and government officials from entering the United States. It was the only law ever passed in America that excluded a specific national group. It remained in effect until 1943.

cholera—deadly infectious disease whose outbreaks often spread out of control.

colliery—coal mine and its plant and outbuildings.

Cossack—warrior peasant from the Ukraine region of Russia. Cossacks were used by the Russian government as police.

cowcatchers—metal frames once used on the front of locomotives to clear the tracks of obstacles.

culm—bits of slate and other rocks that were separated from the coal and discarded.

Custer, George Armstrong—(1839–1876) U.S. army officer. In the Civil War, Custer was an able leader of Union cavalry. He also distinguished himself in a campaign against the Cheyenne. He was killed at the Battle of Little Bighorn.

czar (zahr)—ruler of Russia. This Russian word is from the Latin word *caesar*, meaning "king."

Democratic Party—one of the two major U.S. political parties. It began under Thomas Jefferson but was almost destroyed by arguments over slavery and the Civil War. It revived after 1876 and became the party of the South until very recent times.

depression—severe slowdown in business activity. During a depression, people cannot find jobs, don't have enough money to buy goods, and there is widespread poverty.

discrimination—unfair treatment of a person or group based on negative ideas about such characteristics as skin color, nationality, religion, or gender.

district attorney—official who tries criminal cases in a specific district or area.

Earp (urp), **Wyatt**—(1848–1929) famous lawman in Dodge City, Kansas, and Tombstone, Arizona.

Ellis Island—island in New York Harbor used at the turn of the twentieth century for the processing of immigrants to the United States. About 17 million people came through the Great Hall at Ellis Island between 1892 and 1924, most of them before 1914.

emigrant—one who leaves a country. An immigrant is one who enters a country.

epidemic—rapid spread of a disease so that many people have it at one time.

exposé (EK•spoh•ZAY)—making public of crime, dishonesty, fraud, or something similar.

"Father's a Drunkard and Mother Is Dead"—perhaps the most popular temperance song of the late 1800s. It described the unhappy life of a girl whose family had been destroyed by her father's drinking.

Ghost Dance—late-nineteenth-century religious movement among Indian tribes in the West. An Indian prophet named Wovoka (c. 1858–1932) believed God had chosen him to spread this message. After the massacre at Wounded Knee, the Ghost Dance movement died out.

gold rush—rapid movement of migrants to an area where gold has been discovered. California's gold rush began in 1848, when gold was discovered at Sutter's Mill. Within a year, about 80,000 miners had flooded into the area from all over the world.

Gum San—name, meaning "Gold Mountain," that Chinese people from the Canton area of China gave to California and other areas of the western coast of North America where gold was being mined.

Harlan, John Marshall—(1833–1911) U.S. Supreme Court justice.

harpy—in Greek mythology, a very ugly creature that was part woman and part bird. Harpies were said to steal food and carry off the souls of the dead.

Harte, Bret—(1836–1902) U.S. author who wrote many stories about life in the West.

Holliday, Doc—John Holliday (1850–1887), dentist, gambler, and gunman; friend of the Earps.

Hotchkiss guns—rapid-fire field artillery that fired shells weighing over two pounds with a range of over 4,000 yards.

impeachment—accusation in a legal proceeding of a public official who is said to have behaved improperly in office.

infant mortality rate—percent of babies who die in a given time period. The rate is usually measured in deaths per thousand infants born in a given year.

inquest—judicial inquiry into a matter, usually held before a jury, especially into the cause of a death.

Jim Crow—system of customs and laws that discriminated against African Americans. The name came from a character in minstrel shows, which used a low form of humor to stereotype blacks.

Lease, Mary Elizabeth—(1850–1933) popular Kansas public speaker of the late 1800s. Lease helped a number of Populist candidates, including a governor of Kansas, to win elections.

lice—small, wingless insects that enter the hair or skin of people and animals and suck their blood. Their bites can cause itching, redness, and soreness. They spread very easily under the conditions of overcrowding and lack of sanitary facilities found in the steerage of ships. Lice can carry disease, and their bites can lead to infections.

literacy tests—tests that determine whether a person can read and write. The requirement of literacy tests for voters was a way around the Fifteenth Amendment. It kept many African Americans from voting.

Little Bighorn—Montana river that was the site of a battle on June 25, 1876, between Indians and the U.S. seventh Cavalry. The Sioux and Cheyenne warriors wiped out the government forces.

lynch—to put a person to death, usually by hanging, without a lawful trial. Lynching is most often a mob action.

marshal—U.S. federal law officer.

Memphis *Free Speech*—newspaper edited and partly owned by Ida B. Wells, aimed at an African-American readership in Memphis, Tennessee, and surrounding areas of the South.

Moss, Tom—one of three Memphis men lynched in March 1892; the episode helped spark Ida Wells's anti-lynching work.

muckraker—American journalist or novelist of the early 1900s who exposed social and political evils.

Nation, Carry—(1846–1911) temperance worker who became famous for destroying saloons, first with rocks and bricks and then with hatchets. She was born in Kentucky, but did most of her "smashing" in and around Kansas.

nitroglycerin—explosive liquid used in making dynamite and medicines.

piecework—work that is paid for by the amount of work done, not by the time it takes.

Pinchback, Pinckney Benton Stewart—(1837–1921) first black governor in the United States.

pink paper—The Memphis *Free Speech* was printed on pink paper so people who could not read could identify it easily.

Plessy v. Ferguson—(1896) U.S. Supreme Court decision that permitted states to set up racially separate public services. This decision wasn't reversed until the 1954 *Brown v. Board of Education* decision, which outlawed school segregation.

poll tax—tax that had to be paid before voting. Poll taxes were commonly used in the South to prevent blacks and poor whites from voting. They were outlawed by the Constitution's Twenty-fourth Amendment (1964).

Populists—political party (officially, People's Party) made up mostly of Midwestern farmers. Populists were concerned over low crop prices, crop failures, unfair loan interest rates, and marketing costs. Several Populist candidates were elected to Congress and many to local offices, but the party never received national support.

Prohibition—law against manufacture and sale of alcoholic beverages in the United States.

Promontory—place where the builders of the Central Pacific and Union Pacific railroads met on May 10, 1869, completing the first transcontinental railroad. Promontory is near the Great Salt Lake in Utah. A promontory is a high point of land stretching out into the water.

public facilities—services such as buses, trains, schools, parks, and swimming pools that are usually available for everyone.

quarantined—put into isolation for a period of time to prevent disease from spreading.

Reconstruction—(1865–1877) process after the Civil War involving readmission of the eleven Confederate states. The term is also used to refer to the period when this was done.

Red Cloud—(1822–1909) chief of the Oglala Sioux. In 1866 he led attacks on whites who traveled the Bozeman Trail, a shortcut between Wyoming and Montana to western goldfields. However, after this period he was not involved in warfare with the whites.

registration—putting one's name on a list of qualified voters.

Republican Party—one of the two major U.S. political parties. The Republican Party was founded in 1854 to oppose the extension of slavery. Lincoln was the first Republican president.

Riis (rees)**, Jacob**—(1849–1914) Danish-born U.S. newspaper writer and social reformer.

robber barons—American men of the late 1800s who became powerful in industry or finance, often by illegal means.

Rockefeller, John D.—(1839–1937) U.S. industrialist who entered the oil industry as a young man and built Standard Oil by combining other companies. Later on, Rockefeller set up several charitable foundations

rubles—units of Russian money.

saloon—place where alcoholic drinks are sold and drunk; tavern or bar.

scalawags—insulting term for Southerners who supported Reconstruction. Some had opposed secession and sincerely hoped to reform the South. But others were corrupt and joined the Republican Party for political and financial gain. *Scalawags* originally was a term for worthless cattle.

sentence—punishment decided on by a judge.

sharecroppers—tenant farmers who work the land for a share of the crop minus charges. A sharecropper usually is provided with credit for seed, tools, living quarters, and food.

sheriff—county law officer.

shirtwaist—woman's or girl's blouse that usually has a collar and cuffs.

Sierra Nevada—mountain range in eastern California.

Sioux—group of American Indian tribes living on the plains of the northern United States.

Sitting Bull—(about 1831–1890) chief of the Teton Dakota Sioux and head of the Sioux Nation. Sitting Bull led the Sioux in the last major Indian resistance movement in the United States, defeating government troops at Little Bighorn.

socialism—political system in which workers share in the ownership of farms, factories, and other means of production and also share in the profits.

Statue of Liberty—giant statue of a woman holding a torch that stands in New York Harbor. Unveiled in 1886, it became a beacon of hope for immigrants.

steerage—part of a passenger ship occupied by those traveling at the cheapest rate.

suffrage—right to vote. The movement to get U.S. women the right to vote began with the Seneca Falls Convention (1848) for women's rights, organized by Elizabeth Cady Stanton and Lucretia Mott.

sweatshop—name for a place where workers are employed at low pay for long hours under bad conditions.

temperance movement—organized activity of the 1800s and early 1900s against the sale and drinking of alcoholic drinks.

tenements—buildings in a poor section of a city that are divided into sets of rooms that are occupied by different families.

Tombstone—Arizona mining town that grew rapidly after silver was discovered there in 1877.

Torah—body of Jewish law and tradition; also, the first five books of the Hebrew Bible.

transcontinental—crossing a continent. The transcontinental railroad provided a continuous passage from California to the East Coast.

Vanderbilt, Cornelius—(1794–1877) U.S. businessman who made a fortune in shipping and railroads. Vanderbilt later gave $1 million of his fortune to Vanderbilt University in Nashville, Tennessee.

verdict—decision of a judge or jury in a case of law.

Wall Street—street in New York City on which the major banks and investment houses are located. The term *Wall Street* sometimes is used to symbolize wealthy business interests.

War of 1812—(1812–1814) unpopular conflict with Great Britain. It was a response to shipping restrictions brought about by the British war with France and to the Canadian British arming of the Shawnee chief Tecumseh.

warrant—written order giving authority to do something.

Wells, Miss—Ida B. Wells (1862–1931), newspaper editor who became a crusader for racial justice. She wrote and spoke out against the frequent mob killings of African Americans that were going on in the South.

Acknowledgements

10 © Corbis.
12 Courtesy Library of Congress.
14 Bettman/Corbis.
19 © Harper's Weekly.
21 Courtesy U.S. Patent Office.
25, 26, 29 Courtesy Library of Congress.
34, 38 © The Granger Collection.
43, 48 © Harpers Weekly.
50 © Corbis.
55 © The Granger Collection.
63 Courtesy Library of Congress.
67, 73 © Corbis.
75 © The Granger Collection.
84, 88 © Keystone-Mast Collection, UCR/California Museum of Photography, University of California at Riverside.
94, 98, 102 © Bettman/Corbis.

104, 110 © The Granger Collection.
113, 117, 120 Courtesy Library of Congress.
122, 128 © The Granger Collection.
131 © Tri-Star Boze Publications.
134 Stamp Design © 1994 U.S. Postal Service. Reproduced with permission. All rights reserved.
143 © Bettman/Corbis.
146, 150 © Culver Pictures.
152 © James Mooney/Smithsonian Institute Photos.
161 Courtesy Library of Congress.
164 © James Mooney/Smithsonian Institute Photos.
167, 174, 176, 179 Courtesy Library of Congress.
188 Bettman/Corbis.
191 © The Granger Collection.